A Field Guide To Paranormal Research

Written By B.H. Powell 2024
Copyright 2024

Dedication

This work is dedicated to the memory of Tim King, A great friend, Investigative Researcher and Reporter. Thank you for your love of the field, and for encouraging me to write and publish this book.

Table of Contents

Acknowledgements

Michael Gambino- *Long time personal friend and part of OPHIR's Triumvirate. Intuitive and consultant/Lead Investigator and Researcher*

Bret Edmisten-*Long time friend and part of OPHIR's Triumvirate. Tech specialist and group skeptic. Consultant/Lead Investigator and Researcher (also the guy we send into dark and tight spaces).*

Christopher Califf- *For years of alliance and friendship, and being a trailblazer early on in the Salem/Oregon area and kicking doors open in the area of conducting paranormal research in the local market.*

Joe Campbell- *Founder of "Gotcha Ghost" for making awesome investigative equipment and allowing us to experiment with his new creations.*

Patricia Feeny- *Oregon Department of Human Services for granting access to myself and Tim King to explore and document the underground tunnels at the Oregon State Hospital before the demolition and remodel of the J-Building.*

Staff and Security at Western Oregon University- *For granting us access to Todd Hall and the adjacent cottage.*

Tim and Bonnie King- *Creators of Salem-News.com and several other Media Outlets; for being great friends and always encouraging me to write, and explore my interests, and helping to get my ideas and articles published.*

CCTV Salem- *(Capital Community Television), especially Arlan Robinson, Charles Lewis and Alan Bushong, for airing our videos and the training on, and utilization of their equipment for production purposes.*

And countless others who have played a part in my journey…. I thank you.

Preface

I certainly have my own philosophy, or framework on which I believe everything hangs, and I have formulated it from years of study and the practical application and observation of what I have learned, but I never bring that into an investigation.

This is a problem for many people in terms of research and exposition in any field of subjective study. For example, in the field of paranormal research, there are some who mingle their religious beliefs with whatever they feel, find or experience in the field; oftentimes imposing this, their personal views, onto their clients' situations.

Obviously this approach renders objectivity obsolete. They will make everything they or others experience fit into their own personal paradigm. They are looking rather for confirmation of what they already believe to be true, while negating or overlooking any possible explanations that may not align with their personal views and beliefs.

This type of Researcher believes for the most part, that all souls have a specific destination upon the physical death of the body (Heaven or Hell), so naturally anything hanging around in our world is demonic in nature, an entity whose only goal is to deceive us into thinking they are disincarnate human energy or loved ones who have passed on.

Not to say that this is not a possibility, but should not be the presupposition in all cases.

Another problem in the area of paranormal research is the term "Ghost Hunting." Many groups and organizations use this term interchangeably with the word investigating, which also presents a conflict of interest in the realm of objectivity and says something about the groups founders, members and method, as well as their approach to investigations.

It suggests (to me) that a group such as this is going into situations with a predetermined belief that the place or location is *indeed* haunted already. They are not necessarily looking for logical or mundane explanations, they are going into the investigation already expecting that "ghosts" are responsible for whatever may or may not be happening.

These are usually thrill-seekers, out looking for a good scare. As I have said, this is not conducive to actual research, which needs to be approached objectively. As a matter of fact, in conducting investigations and following up on inquiries from potential clients, we have systems in place.

Only a couple of the group members who are greatly trusted would be invited to the initial contact with the Client (including our then resident Psychologist). We would meet up after the initial contact, and discuss our findings and impressions of the Client and details surrounding their predicament, and then decide if we wanted to proceed with an actual investigation involving the whole team, and conduct an investigation either collectively, or in part.

The exact location was always withheld from members (especially those claiming to have psychic or mediumistic abilities) to avoid them doing their own research beforehand, which could potentially "taint" or "influence" their experiences at said location.

For example: One such early on team member had done some research into a location we were supposed to be investigating and came to learn that someone, a female, had purportedly committed suicide at the location by hanging herself.

At one point during the night, She had led other group members to a tree in the backyard, and began claiming to feel an overwhelming rush of emotions, and began to feel as if her airway was obstructed.

"Feels like I can't breathe, like I'm being choked" she said, which immediately made me suspicious, being that she had revealed that she did some research into the claims surrounding the property prior to the investigation while we were enroute to the location.

Another obvious problem is properly obtaining permissions. Many groups or bands of individuals trespass in the name of paranormal research, and in some cases, vandalize. I remember trying to get access to locations but the Owners or Proprietors of the properties were apprehensive because people representing themselves as ghost hunters had entered illegally and spray painted "I Love Ghosts" on the interior walls as a sign that they had been there.

These types of groups generally frequent cemeteries and other unoccupied locations (abandoned buildings etc.). No Trespassing signs exist for a reason! Sometimes for your own personal safety, as in instances of weak or deteriorating structures and roofs that may be close to caving in.

Also, many times locations such as these are not suitable for investigations because of noise pollution. Many cemeteries are located on or near public roads and surrounding neighborhoods. You will experience everything from passing cars to dogs barking, making it nearly impossible to get clean audio recordings.

Another issue (in my opinion) is that many people just starting out in the field face the initial problem of not having access to locations in which to actively investigate, so they naturally start conducting investigations in their own homes, and the homes of other members.

This is not advised! I would not conduct inquiries at my own place of residence. If you believe nothing will come from the investigation, why do it? I personally know someone who started holding EVP sessions at their personal residence and had to eventually move out because, well... they began experiencing the very things they were looking for.

Using electronic recording devices during an EVP session is much like using a Ouija Board in a question and answer session. If you start asking general questions into an open environment you are inviting things to communicate with you, only using a digital medium instead of the board.

Eventually, because of intent and repetition, you WILL make contact with *something*, but do you really want to invite that energy into your personal residence?

It is imperative therefore, if we are to be taken seriously *at all* as researchers, that we avoid such practices and seek to separate ourselves from groups such as these.

My interest in the supernatural started as a child. *** Later, as an adult, I made the decision to delve a little more deeply. I studied various strands of occult teachings and philosophy independently at first, eventually gaining access to the more structured writings, teachings and practices of various "Mystery Schools" and Esoteric Societies.

I eventually became a Freemason, hoping I could find answers there, but was disappointed to find that for the most part, the majority of the members of the Lodge were of the same levels of intellect and insight as any other common section of society, and I had a greater degree of knowledge on Symbolism and Esotericism walking through the door for the first time than many of them had obtained after years of membership. In fact, for most of them it was just a club comprised of guys looking for an excuse to get out of the house (and away from their wives).

Knowledge in the lodge was just as fleeting as it was anywhere else, and the few you could find with any degree of understanding had their heads so far up their own asses that spending any amount of time with them in conversation was almost unbearable. Similar to modern church-goers, people would religiously quote scripture and ceremony, but did not have their own thoughts or understanding on the subject matter well enough to explain or expound on the material in their own words.

Started looking after moving to Oregon in 2005. Found a couple of groups, they were disorganized, but I found a few people that I thought would work out. Carefully picking members and events we participated in… PK Playhouse Halloween radio. Willamette University Annabelle, Monks, Zaffis.

Simplified versions of cleansing rituals, materials. Psychology of cleansing rituals… sage vs frankincense etc.

Founded OPHIR in 2007, formed and organized, sought members, phony psychics, members, classes at Chemeketa, Radio, video etc.

Whispers in ear, rice krispies, slow motion, friends. Grandmother experience, kerril, Sara, candles.

The following is a collection of writings I have had published over the course of the last decade or so. The Ghost stories are all based on events that, according to the individuals that shared them with me, are true. They have been shared with me over the past few years by people I have met in person, others have been shared with me through email correspondences over the years. I have a few experiences of my

13

own but I choose to keep those private for the time being. The articles are based on research I have done, sometimes prompted by my own curiosity, other times by the need to find logical explanations for conditions presented by cases we were researching. I have added additional information or notes to some of the articles making them different from when they were originally published. For some paranormal enthusiasts, a couple of the articles may be slightly familiar as many of the articles have been shared by various paranormal research groups over the years; on websites and in forums across the internet.

I will be the first to admit that most of the claims and locations we visited as a group yielded no results or findings at all, but there have been a few that left more questions than answers. When I first moved to Oregon, I had set out to find a group that was actively seeking out and investigating reportedly "haunted" locations, I found one. I contacted the group and was invited to tag along and participate in one of their investigations. It was an interesting experience but I immediately identified certain flaws in their approach and method; namely, they seemed to go into the cases with the supposition that these locations were *indeed* haunted before even visiting the site or doing any real research on the location at all. They were also conducting many of these investigations outdoors and with permission from the property owners. After a couple of outings with these groups, I decided to start my own with a couple of individuals that I came into contact with from other various groups. People who seemed sane and objective. Since the subject of paranormal research or parapsychology is looked down upon, I carefully tried to choose reputable members for the group and build a well-rounded team of individuals including a Psychologist, a Lawyer, an Investigative Reporter, a Historian and a Physicist, as well skeptics and believers alike.

Eventually, I was invited to teach a course at a local community College that was listed under the category of "Irregular psychology" called Introduction to Paranormal Research, or, to attract students, "Ghost Hunting 101." The course ran for a few weeks and culminated in a full on investigation at a location that was publicly known and believed to be haunted. We were also invited to do two radio programs and were contacted by Zodiac Productions to possibly begin production for a pilot of a television show for the SYFY channel based on an article I had published entitled "Buyer Beware" which is included in this body of work.

I am not a complete skeptic where paranormal occurrences are concerned, but as I have always said, I do not necessarily believe the Client who claims that the doorway to Narnia is in their closet.

Introduction

For me personally, growing up in my parents' house as a child, there were always tales of ghosts and strange occurrences. Being of West Indian descent, this was, for the most part, dinner table conversation for us.

There were stories of deceased relatives who were still heard arguing in their now abandoned home where the front yard was now littered with overgrown grass, shrubs and trees; there were stories of "Voodoo" rituals and spells that had been cast on family members in the past, mysterious black dogs and giant crows guarding my grandfather's house.

My grandmother was even said to have done battle with the village "witch," whom she is rumored to have exposed by saving the swept up dust from the house for three days, then beating it with a scourge she fashioned by braiding three young branches together. It is said that the next day, the suspected woman was bedridden, overcome with pain and her body covered in welts and bruises.

On the other hand, aside from being spiritually inclined, my mother was also religious. She made sure we went to church and attended Sunday school where I heard accounts of angelic (and demonic) encounters and divine intervention.

At about age 8 or 9, while battling with a case of pneumonia, I had my first "Out-of-Body Experience." I distinctly remember lying on the bed and feeling "floaty." After a couple of minutes, I was above myself looking down at my motionless body. I saw my mother walk into my bedroom to check on me; she placed her hand on my forehead, removed a dish from my bedside, and walked out.

After I felt better I told her about the experience and she told me that this was a fairly common thing, that it has happened to others and that some people could even control it. She had a couple of books on the subject, (mainly written by Shirley MacLaine), and gave me access to them.

Under the circumstances and in these conditions, I naturally developed an acute interest in the unseen and unknown from a very early age. I obtained my first book on the paranormal at age 10; it was titled, "Into the Unknown" by Readers Digest, published in 1981, which I still have in my possession to this day, some 40 years-plus later. To my delight, the book not only covered ghosts and "monsters," but it also discussed some of the subjects that I found more interesting like ESP and precognition, Black Magic and Divination, UFO's and out-of-body experiences. I was hooked! And so my love affair with the field of the paranormal began.

Interestingly, I *also* had (and still have) an intense respect and love for religion. I was not (and am not) particularly religious mind you, but I have always been in awe of the reverence dedicated to the sacraments and teachings of ALL religions, everything from the art and architecture to the language and symbolism, all spoke to me on a much deeper level than the actual words that made up the stories ever could. There was definitely (to me) more going on than met the eye... as far as my perception and instincts were concerned anyway.

Much to my frustration however, conventional religion (Christianity in particular), told me that the worlds of my two loves were irreconcilable; the paranormal, ghosts, divination, Ouija boards, out of body experiences etc. were all "evil" and "of the devil". Well, I myself personally had an out-of-body experience, and there was nothing diabolical or malevolent about it!

Perplexed with the answers I received and determined to find my own way, I have spent years studying religion and esoteric symbolism and it is an ongoing journey for me. I sought out people with similar interests and experiences and eventually began actively seeking out and investigating accounts of paranormal phenomena and strange or inexplicable occurrences on my own as a result.

Because of my continued research, I am constantly forced to re-evaluate, reconsider and modify my philosophy based on the things that I (and others) see, learn and experience around me.

To continue the work, I founded a paranormal research team based in Salem, Oregon, in an attempt to find the answers to the unresolved questions that I believe fascinate us all.

Thus far, no one has been able to answer questions pertaining to the after-life, and we are all seeking answers pertaining to *why* we are here, *where* we come from and *where* we are going, but this barely scratches the surface on defining the field of paranormal research and all it encompasses.

So my personal journey continued. This was not just limited to understanding ghosts and such, I was in search of mystical knowledge as a natural result: Later, as an adult, I made the decision to delve a little more deeply, I studied various strands of occult teachings and philosophy independently at first, eventually gaining access to the more structured writings, teachings and practices of various "Mystery Schools" and Esoteric Societies. I eventually became a Freemason, hoping I could find answers there, but was disappointed to find that for the most part, the majority of the members of the Lodge were of the same levels of intellect and insight as any other common section of society, by this time in my life, as a result of independent study, I had a greater degree of knowledge on Symbolism and Esotericism walking through the door for the first time than many of them had obtained after years of membership. In fact, for most of them it was just a club composed of guys looking for an excuse to get out of the house (and away from their wives) Similar to modern church-goers, people would religiously quote rite and ceremony, but did not

have their own thoughts or
understanding on the subject matter
well enough to explain or expound on
the material in their own words. The
articles are based on research I have
done, sometimes prompted by my own
curiosity, other times by the need to
find logical explanations for
conditions presented by cases we were
researching. I have added additional
information or notes to some of the
articles making them different from
when they were originally published.
For some paranormal enthusiasts, a
couple of the articles may be slightly
familiar as many of the articles have
been shared by various other paranormal
research groups over the years on
websites and in forums across the web.

I will be the first to admit that most
of the claims and locations we visited
as a group yielded no results or
findings at all, but there have been a
few that left more questions than
answers. When I first moved to Oregon,
I had set out to find a group that was
actively seeking and investigating
reportedly haunted locations, and I
found one. I contacted the group and
was invited to tag along and
participate in one of their
investigations. It was an interesting
experience but I immediately identified

certain flaws in their approach and method; namely, they seemed to go into the cases with the predisposition that these locations were already *indeed* haunted before visiting the site or doing any preliminary research on the location at all. They were also conducting many of these investigations outdoors and without permission from the property owners. After a couple of outings with these groups, I decided to start my own research group with a couple of individuals that I came into contact with from other various groups. People who seemed sane and objective.

Since the subject of paranormal research or parapsychology is so looked down upon, I carefully tried to choose reputable members for the group and build a well-rounded team of individuals including a Psychologist, a Lawyer, an Investigative Reporter, a Historian and a Physicist, an Enforcement Officer, as well skeptics and believers alike.

Eventually, I was invited to teach a course at a local community College that was listed under the category of "Irregular psychology" called Introduction to Paranormal Research, or, to attract students, "Ghost Hunting 101." The course ran for a few weeks and culminated in a full-on

investigation at a location that was
publicly known and believed to be
haunted. We were also invited to do two
radio programs and were contacted by
Zodiac Productions to possibly begin
production for a pilot of a television
show for the SYFY channel based on an
article I had published entitled "Buyer
Beware" which is included in this body
of work.

I am not a complete skeptic where
paranormal occurrences are concerned,
but as I have always said, I do not
necessarily believe the Client who
claims that the doorway to Narnia is in
their closet.

Beginnings of Modern Paranormal Research

The modern infatuation with psychic phenomena and paranormal activity started with the Spiritualist Movement in or around 1848 in Hydesville New York with the Fox sisters. Margaretta (Maggie) and Catherine (Kate) were the initial catalysts of the movement, but they also had an older sister named Leah, who later became a sort of manager to them and took control of their careers by booking events and readings to paying audiences and private clients.

They lived in their family home with their parents in upstate New York. In March of 1848, when they were about 14 and 11 years old respectively, they told their parents that they had been communicating with a spirit through tapping sounds. The sisters claimed that they heard knocks on the furniture and walls of their bedroom at night.

The girls then demonstrated this for their parents. Supposedly their mother asked out loud, "How many children do I have?," and she reportedly heard the correct number of knocks. Soon the neighbors heard the rumors and word spread like wildfire that the sisters could communicate with the dead.

Just a year later, the Fox sisters were hosting public demonstrations to paying audiences. In November of 1849 with the help of their sister Leah, they held a public demonstration of their abilities at Corinthian Hall in Rochester New York. There were around 400 paying witnesses in attendance and the event was covered by local newspapers of the day. Soon the girls were hosting demonstrations in New York City and the Spiritualist Movement was born.

This inspired many new psychics and mediums to spring up out of the woodwork. What made matters worse was that in 1861, during the height of the Spiritualist Craze, the United States entered into the Civil War.

With the loss of so many young men to the war, Spiritualism offered a new sense of hope to newly widowed wives and mothers looking for closure with their deceased loved ones… and there were plenty of new mediums around to capitalize off of them.

Even First Lady, Mary Todd Lincoln reportedly held seances at the White House during Lincoln's Presidency in an attempt to make contact with her three dead children (not war related).

Spiritualists started using all types of parlor tricks to swindle money out of clients, taking advantage of their distress. I am not implying that all mediums and psychics are or were frauds, but charlatanism was definitely at an all time high. In so much that arguably the very first paranormal research organization ever, called The Ghost Club, was formed in London in 1862.

Ghost club would investigate spiritualist phenomena and meet up to discuss their thoughts and findings. Members included Charles Dickens, Sir Arthur Conan Doyle, W.B Yeats and many other public and professional figures; though it operated as more of a secret society, and did not publish the names of its members.

Ghost Club disbanded in the 1870's not long after the death of Charles Dickens, but was revitalized on November 1, 1882. The new Ghost Club was mainly composed of believers in psychic phenomena, so to counter that, an Organization called SPR (Society for Psychical Research) was also formed the same year, and attracted the likes of Mark Twain.

SPR was the first organization of its kind:

"Attempting to understand events and abilities commonly described as psychic or paranormal."

They described themselves as *"The first society to conduct organized and scholarly scientific research on human experiences that challenge contemporary scientific models,"* and there were no core beliefs. Unlike Ghost Club, members all had their own personal opinions and beliefs concerning the nature of the cases they investigate.

One member of SPR was actually
sent to India to investigate Helena
Petrovna Blavatski, as she had founded
the Theosophical Society in 1875 which
was gaining popularity, and she claimed
to have psychic powers. SPR's findings
in the investigation were inconclusive
or never proven.

Though he never joined a society
or club, Harry Houdini was very
skeptical of psychic abilities and
devoted a good portion of his life
attempting to discredit Spiritualists
and prove their abilities to be nothing
more than smoke in mirrors. With
cameras becoming available to the
general public, one of the methods used
by Spiritualists was "spirit
photography." This was done mainly by
causing a double exposure during the
photography and development process
similar to a technique called Pepper's
Ghost, in which the likeness or image
of an item or person off stage was made
to appear as it was on stage or in
front of the audience during plays or
in the cinema.

As photographers learned more
about film development and double
exposure, spirit photography became

more and more popular. In fact, one such photographer supplied Mary Tood Lincoln with a picture of herself with her then dead husband seemingly behind her.

In later times Houdini attempted to discredit this method by furnishing a picture of himself with the late Abraham Lincoln, which he was able to produce.

During his lifetime he had made a pact with his wife Bess, that if it were at all possible, after his death, he would come back and make contact with her. Being the great escape artist that he was, she was positive that if anyone could break through, it would be her husband. For the following 10 years after his death, she held a seance every October 31st (the date of his demise)hoping that her dead husband would have a message from beyond the grave. In 1936 she made her final attempt, after a decade had passed without success, she stopped.

Earlier that same year, *Harry Price (known as the father of modern ghost hunting) published a work entitled, "Confessions of a Ghost

Hunter," bringing paranormal investigation to the forefront of people's imaginations. His book not only covered details of his research but also introduced the public to things like contact with alien beings, poltergeist activity, precognition, fire-walking and other feats performed by people with seemingly remarkable natural abilities.

In 1925 Price started the National Laboratory of Psychical Research after falling into a number of disagreements with SPR and in 1934 the University of London built and equipped a Department of Psychical Research, giving Price full access and a place to keep his collection of haunted artifacts and inventions he had built to aid in his research.

Also being a writer, Price published many other works including research papers, giving him the reputation of a "scientific ghost hunter" and Britain's most famous investigator of ghosts and hauntings.

Four years after his death in 1948, Edward and Lorraine Warren burst into public view by forming the New

England Society for Psychic Research (NESPR) which is now considered the oldest ghost hunting group in New England, and possibly the United States. Edward was a self taught author, demonologist and lecturer while Lorraine, his wife, claimed to be clairvoyant and a *trance medium.

The Warrens claimed to have investigated thousands of cases during their careers as paranormal researchers and published many books about their research. Ed claimed to be one of only seven *demonologists in the United States and trained others in this discipline, including John Zaffis, who has picked up the Warrens mantle in modern times. Some of their more well known cases have been made into movies such as the Amityville Horror (Based on the story of the DeFeo Family in Long Island New York), Annabelle (a Raggedy Anne doll first given to a Nurse in Hartford CT), and The Conjuring (based off of a case in Harrisville Rhode Island).

Tools and Methodology

As time progressed and people got more sophisticated (and exposed to the idea of observing and measuring paranormal activity) tools began to become commonplace with hobbyists and serious investigators alike.

Here I include a general but not complete list of some of the tools and methods used by researchers in early, and modern times. It should be noted that most equipment is *not* made specifically for paranormal research, but other applications that have been incorporated into the field for the need of recordable and observable information in an attempt to apply scientific methods to research.

Automatic Writing- Or psychography as it is called by more serious researchers, is the act of a person, usually with assumed psychic abilities, writing on a piece of paper without thinking or consciously writing. Over the years this has been done by having the Medium hold a pencil on a sheet of paper and allowing a spirit to move or manipulate the hand, or by the use of a planchette.

Photography- photography is used in an attempt to capture images of ghosts on film or digitally. It is believed that the lens of the camera may be able to pick up things in our light spectrum unseen by the human eye, or simply to capture an event (such as an object being moved or levitated, a wisp of "*plasma" or, mostly commonly, *orbs).

In 1862 a man named William Mumler made public a photograph that he took that featured the image of his cousin who had been dead for 12 years. The resulting media coverage caused him to abandon his current business as a jewelry engraver, and became a successful Spirit Photographic Medium as he called it.

It was Mumler who gave Mary Tood Lincoln the photograph of herself with her assassinated husband, which became his most famous photograph.

Ouija Boards-Though spirit boards can be found reported much earlier in history, (1100 C.E. in China) about the

same time period that the Spiritualist
Movement was taking hold.

In 1890 Charles Kennard and Elijah
Bond applied for a patent on the spirit
board, which was initially denied.
He then travelled to Washington D.C.
where he persuaded the Chief Patent
Officer to try the board out for
himself. Allegedly, he asked the board
to spell out his name, which it did and
Bond was granted the patent in 1891.

Bond and Kennard formed The
Kennard Novelty Company for the sole
purpose of producing Spirit Boards.
Soon they had factories in Baltimore,
New York, Chicago and London. The
company was later bought by an employee
of Bond's, a man named William Flud who
changed the name to Ouija Board.

Flud died in 1927 after falling
off of the roof of a brand new factory,
which he claimed the board told him to
build. Ouija boards became not only a
staple and widely used tool among
Spiritualists, but they were now
accessible to the general public at
large and were marketed as a board game
for adults and children alike.

Crystals- Highly popular in the "New Age Movement" crystals are believed to be naturally tuned to certain frequencies, each having its own unique properties. They are used sometimes to amplify or diminish certain abilities in the wearer, aid in the communication with spirits or "guides," and for protection.

It is commonly believed that certain frequencies can negate, or neutralize others, so crystals are sometimes used to ward off negative energy. Interestingly, crystals, called Quartz Crystals, are used in modern communication equipment like cell phones, satellites, and long range communication devices (walkie talkies) to provide reliable and stable data transmissions across wireless networks.

Dowsing Rods- Sometimes called Witching Sticks or Divination Rods are usually either a pair of thin metal "L" shaped rods, or a "Y" shaped stick.

Originally used to locate ground water for the digging of wells, they have also been used in an attempt to find the locations of precious metals and stones, petroleum deposits, buried treasure, gravesites and Leylines.

In paranormal research, some investigators utilize dowsing rods to detect shifts in energy believed to point to the presence of a spirit or entity.

Seance- The most common way of trying to contact the spirit world were seances. This was generally done through the use of a Spiritual Medium. Typically they are held by people who were close to the deceased, and for more effectiveness, a personal possession of the deceased is used to attract the spirit that participants are attempting to make contact with.

There are different methods used by Mediums to achieve contact with spirits, the first one we will discuss is called "Trance Mediumship." This is when the Medium goes into a trance like state prior to contact, allowing the spirit to speak through them. These tend to employ video recordings of the session or, in some cases, a person taking dictation of the events as they usually do not remember what has transpired while they were in the trance state.

Another form is Channeling. In this method the Medium acts as a conduit for the spirit, in some cases even adopting the mannerisms and accent of the deceased. The "consciousness" of the spirit animates the Medium, who basically has "stepped aside" allowing the spirit to utilize their physical vehicle.

Widely familiar today is the group session method, where the Medium is in front of an audience. Though this is not considered a proper seance, as the Medium is not sitting, it is probably the most familiar version of a modern seance.

Flour- Simply enough, flour has been used to detect things like footprints, and is sometimes placed on or around an object of interest to see if they have been moved while not being directly observed.

Kirlian Photography, or Electrography- Popularized around 1939 by Seymon Kirlian, this method was used in an attempt to capture an image of the subject's aura.

The technique was discovered by Kirlian accidentally while he was experimenting with photos and the plates that were used to capture images before photographic film was developed. He found that if he ran voltage through the subject at the time of taking the picture, that an electrical discharge was visible in the photograph.

Notebook and Pen- Used to record findings and observations and to take notes for future comparison and documentation of the timeline of events,

Modern Equipment

EMF Meters- Used to detect changes or fluctuations in the immediate Electromagnetic field in or around a particular environment. It is believed that if a spirit or entity is present, it will be observable as the going theory is that spirits are comprised of energy, thus giving off their own electromagnetic field,

Full Spectrum Cameras- Cameras that have had the filters removed from the lenses and or processors (in the cast of modern digital cameras) to allow both or either the infrared and ultraviolet light be captured by the camera.

Digital Voice Recorders- Used during investigations in an attempt to capture EVP's (electronic voice phenomena). Popularized by a man named Konstantis Raudive in the 1970's, Investigators generally ask specific questions, usually pertinent to the conditions and details surrounding the case they are working on in hopes of receiving answers.

The theory is that the digital recording device may be able to pick up voices insensible to human ears. Results can be checked on the spot by playing back the recording after a line of questioning, but typically the digital files are uploaded to an audio editing program for closer inspection post investigation.

Closed Circuit Video Cameras- Used to document activity in a general area, or several areas in an attempt to capture evidence of anomalous activity that may not have been observed or observable by researchers at the time of occurrence. Also enabling the ability to go back and reexamine the footage after the investigation is complete.

Laser Grids- Laser grids are used to detect movement, during or post investigation through the observance of "breaks" in the grid. Generally used to detect the presence or movement of shadow entities.

Trigger Objects-Trigger objects are used to solicit a response from one or more subjects of an investigation, generally in cases of intelligent hauntings. Dolls, toys or other personal effects that may have belonged to, or believed to have been somehow related to the circumstances surrounding a haunting or person now deceased.

Mediums- Mediums act as intermediaries between the living and the spirit world. They are more so incorporated into paranormal investigations today than ever before. Many groups either recruit them to assist on cases they are working, or have a dedicated member that is a medium.

Ghost Box- Ghost boxes, also known as a Frank Box (named after its inventor, Frank Sumption) is basically a radio that has had certain capacitors and circuitry removed so that it continuously "scans" the radio broadcast spectrum, never locking in on one particular station or signal.

What you get is mostly *white noise with a random hint or piece of a broadcast here and there, as if you were continually just turning the dial. The theory is that ghosts or spirits can utilize the frequencies to communicate with observers, much like Bumblebee uses his radio to communicate with Sam Witwicky in the movie The Transformers.

Ovilus- The Ovilus works similarly to the ghost box except instead of utilizing radio signals, it uses ambient EMF frequencies and converts them into words.

I personally have witnessed some very interesting results using the Ovilus in the field on numerous investigations. The device is pre-programed with a growing database of words. When it detects changes in the surrounding electromagnetic field (and sometimes, changes in temperature) in a particular environment it converts this into a word or words that are believed to be manipulatable by spirits to communicate with researchers.

Parabolic Microphone- Not commonly seen in modern investigations, parabolic microphones are designed to collect, focus and magnify soundwaves by means of a satellite dish shaped apparatus that direct the sounds into a transducer. The sounds can then be heard through a set of headphones.

They are directional, meaning they will only pick up sounds coming from the direction in which the dish is pointed.

Night Vision Goggles- IR (infrared) goggles or binoculars allow the user to see in the dark. The main problem is that they are only beneficial to the wearer, they generally only work in real time observation and do not capture images that can be saved and examined by others.

With the availability of IR and full spectrum video recorders, night vision goggles are generally no longer used in investigations; but they can be more effective in outdoor settings than cameras with IR technology.

Ambient Temperature Readers- Used to detect changes in temperature in an immediate area. The theory being that the presence of a spirit can be announced or accompanied by a sudden drop in temperature, or "cold spots" which can move about a space, much like electromagnetic fields have been observed to do in certain cases.

Pendulums- Pendulums were used by some early researchers to receive answers to questions before the invention of voice recorders. It operates under the premise that spirits have the ability to manipulate physical objects, if so inclined.

The pendulum was held between the thumb and forefinger and allowed to hang freely. The operator would generally ask questions like, "Is there anyone here with us," to establish a method for answering questions, for example: the pendulum may swing or spin to the left or right, which would be established as the indication of a positive answer, or "yes."

Likewise movement in the opposite direction in response to a question would be interpreted to indicate a negative answer, or "no."

Research Papers

The following section is comprised of various articles and research notes I have taken over the last few years on various subjects while conducting investigations and exploration of various subjects.

I have included examples from real cases we have been involved with where I felt the information was pertinent or relative. Again I do not share the names or identities of those involved.

In all examples taken from cases it was the client who initiated contact with us in regards to what they believed may have been occurring in their homes or businesses, or with their loved ones.

Creating A Ghost

In 1972, members from the Toronto Society for Psychical Research (TSPR), directed by Dr. A.R.G. Owen conducted an experiment to see if they could create a ghost.

They did this by first creating a fictional character, which they named Philip Aylesford. They then created a background story for Philip, fashioning him an English Aristocrat who lived in Europe during the late Renaissance period. Here is a sample of what they came up with:

"Philip was an aristocratic Englishman, living in the middle 1600s at the time of Oliver Cromwell. He had been a supporter of the King, and was a Catholic. He was married to a beautiful but cold and frigid wife, Dorothea, the daughter of a neighboring Nobleman.

One day when out riding on the boundaries of his estates Philip came across a gypsy encampment and saw there a beautiful dark-eyed, raven-haired gypsy girl, Margo, and fell instantly in love with her. He brought her back secretly to live in the gatehouse, near the stables of Diddington Manor - his family home.

For some time he kept his love-nest secret, but eventually Dorothea, realizing he was keeping someone else there, found Margo, and accused her of witchcraft and stealing her husband.

Philip was too scared of losing his reputation and his possessions to protest at the trial of Margo, and she was convicted of witchcraft and burned at the stake.

Philip was subsequently stricken with remorse that he had not tried to defend Margo and used to pace the battlements of Diddington in despair. Finally, one morning his body was found at the bottom of the battlements, whence he had cast himself in a fit of agony and remorse."

The group of researchers then came up with a portrait or likeness for Philip to help make him seem even more authentic to them, bringing him to life in a sense… So with a background story in place and a portrait of him the experiment could begin.

"Philip Aylesford"

In September 1972 the group began to hold informal sittings or meetings in which they would concentrate on Philip and discuss his life to try to expand on his story and add details to his early life, making him seem as real as possible in their minds.

They practiced visualizing him, holding their sittings in fully lit rooms, this went on for a time with no real or measurable results so the group decided to change their technique and incorporate more metaphysical or spiritualistic elements to the experiments.

The sittings began to resemble séances by candlelight, they sat around the table and surrounded themselves with pictures of the type of castle they imagined Philip would have lived in and items from the time period in which they imagined he would have lived, in the hopes of soliciting some effect.

Not long afterwards, during one evening session the group received its very first communication from Phillip in the form of a distinct knock or rap on the table.

Before long the group was asking questions and receiving answers using the basic, one rap for yes, two for no format. They received positive responses from Philip after the group asked if it was him who was with them at this time.

The sessions really picked up from that point on, through the table rapping method the group learned more about Philip, finding out more about his life, his likes and dislikes and his views and preferences. The table was even reported to move on some occasions, sliding from side to side, and dancing on one leg even though it was on a thick carpet.

It was even claimed that the table had chased someone across the room all the while the group's hands were clear of the table when this occurred.

Although Philip could accurately answer questions about events and people from his time period, it did not seem that he presented any information that at least one member of the group was already aware of. Philip's responses seemed to come from their own subconscious minds collectively, as if he were able to "tap into" them.

This is a phenomenon that has been used by Occultists over the years to affect various reasons, sometimes to control others, other times to produce a desired effect or result.

The most basic example would be that of the *Golem: In Jewish Folklore, the Golem is a being created from inanimate material [such as soil or clay] and brought to life through a magical ritual.

The Golem was then given a job or purpose for the sake of bridling the energy imparted to it. Though other cultures shared similar beliefs and practices, such as the Greeks and Czechs, there is to this day a Golem Museum in the Jewish Quarter of Prague (Spain) which displays hominid figures that are believed to have been used for such purposes in the past.

According to one version of the Golem legend of Prague, during the

1500's, the city's Jews, were being violently persecuted and falsely accused of using the blood of Christians to perform their rituals.

To protect the Jewish community, Rabbi Judah Loew built a Golem out of clay from the banks of the Vltava River. He used his knowledge of *kabbalah and mysticism to bring it to life and inscribed the Hebrew word "emet" [meaning truth] across the creature's forehead.

The Golem, whom he called Josef, patrolled the ghetto to protect it from ill-intended outsiders. Eventually, the Golem is said to have ultimately gone on a murderous rampage, and turned against the community he was created to protect.

Rabbi Loew smeared clay on the Golem's forehead, covering or erasing the first letter written across its forehead turning the word "emet" [truth] into "met," which is the Hebrew word for death, and put the creature to rest in the attic of the old New Synagogue.

Similarly, there is a "spiritual" counterpart to the Golem, this is known as an *Egregore. An egregore is an occult concept best described as a "thoughtform" or "collective group mind;" an autonomous psychic entity made up by and of, and often influencing, the thoughts of a group of people.

Occultists have employed the use and concept of the egregore for various reasons. In some cases the thought form can be used to carry out or begin the process of manifesting a particular result that needs to be initiated in a less dense realm before it can be realized in the physical world.

For example: To bring illness or misfortune on a particular individual or group. Those who are familiar with practices such as Reiki will know what this means, since diseases are said to "be seen" or show up in the auric body before physically manifesting or beginning to show symptoms in the physical body.

Egregores are also oftentimes used by various religious or spiritual groups, or their leadership (intentionally or unintentionally), unbeknownst to the regular members who have not been brought into the inner circle of said group.

When the members of such a group, as in a Cult for example, have a particular Deity or god that they praise/worship, the constant focus and mental energy given to the Deity by the group, energizes it.

What was once a thoughtform, overtime, becomes animated by the group's energy and devotion. This is the same *principle* (the power of thought) that comes into play, and I believe the basis of the new age way of thinking concerning manifesting things in your life; As Bob Proctor said during his segment in "The Secret," thoughts become things.

Video recordings of TSPR's experiments in creating Philip and of some of the group's sessions are archived online and can be easily found with a web search.

Range of Light Frequencies

seeing the unseen

The term "full spectrum light" refers to the entire light spectrum including colors both visible and invisible to the human eye, from ultraviolet (around 300 nm) to Infrared (around 1100 nm).

Between these invisible ranges are the visible spectrums that most of us can see with our eyes. All color is actually the result of vibration. The entire spectrum of visible light vibrates at frequencies between about 400 nm to 800 nm (nanometers).

The total light spectrum is much larger than what we are able to see. In fact, visible light is only a tiny fraction of the entire spectrum. The light that we can see with our eyes is known as "white light". It is a combination of all the visible colors of the light spectrum.

Do you remember the mnemonic we learned in school, Roy G. Biv? These letters represent the visible colors of the light spectrum or the colors we see in the rainbow, in their proper order.

Red, Orange, Yellow, Green, Blue,
Indigo and Violet; these are the
frequencies (or colors) that are
visible to us in our light spectrum ...
notice I emphasized 'visible'.

Violet: 400 - 420 nm
Indigo: 420 - 440 nm
Blue: 440 - 490 nm
Green: 490 - 570 nm
Yellow: 570 - 585 nm
Orange: 585 - 620 nm
Red: 620 - 780 nm

**Vibration in
nanometers**

There are also the two extreme
ends of the color spectrum, which we
cannot see, the extreme left and right
ends of the field. Beyond red is
infrared, and on the other end there is
ultra violet.

The chart below shows the
frequencies at which the colors visible
to us within the light spectrum
vibrate.

So these different vibrational
rates are picked up and detected by our
eyes as colors. Higher numbers signify
longer wavelengths, which translate

into a slower vibrational rate or frequency, the lower the number, the shorter the wave and higher the frequency.

The lowest frequency of light we can see appears as red, and the highest appears as violet, but as we said, the entire spectrum of light is much larger than this (300 to 1100 nm).

While we humans cannot see within the infrared or ultraviolet areas of the light spectrum with our eyes, animals and insects can.

This may account for why animals have been reported in the past to seem to react to things that aren't there.

Full spectrum light and its applications in paranormal research:

It is hypothesized that since everything vibrates at various rates, that entities, spirits, ghosts etc may be more visible in other areas of the light spectrum than the normal narrow range of light visible to us.

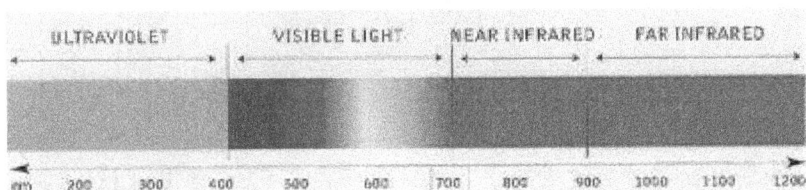

Color Spectrum

Also, since a spirit is believed to be comprised of energy, if that energy vibrates at rates of a higher or lower frequency than our own, then we may be able to capture an image of them if we shoot or record with a camera equipped to pick up things that are present in those ends of the spectrum.

Joe Campbell, a developer and inventor of experimental and modified equipment geared toward paranormal research, actually converts cameras, both still and video, to capture and record images in the full light spectrum.

About which Joe says, *"All cameras are sensitive to the invisible spectrums of light and can register this light via their sensitive CMOS (complementary metal oxide semiconductor) or CCD (charge coupled device) sensor. Both types of imagers convert light into an electric charge and process it into electronic signals.*

Manufacturers install various components that block IR and UV light as these cause undesirable effects in color photography. Generally, a camera is converted to full spectrum by removing these components thus allowing the sensor to process light waves otherwise blocked by the filters." But how does this relate to paranormal research?

In simplest terms, if a "ghost" is made of energy and that energy vibrates at either lower or higher frequency levels than our own, then we should be able to "access" them within these energy fields. If those energy fields correlate to the frequency ranges of either ultraviolet or infrared light, then photographing these light waves should allow that energy to be seen and recorded."

Paranormal Research groups around the country, including members from the popular television show "Ghost Hunters", and "Ghost Adventures" seek after Joe's equipment.

Night vision, which has been in use by paranormal investigators for a number of years now, views the infrared spectrum of light, and standard flash photography captures the visible spectrum of light; so it only seems natural that the ultraviolet end of the spectrum would be explored and incorporated into the realm of paranormal research.

After all, if ghostly apparitions and spectral anomalies can be captured

in IR and visible light then they ought
to be able to be detected in UV, and if
so... *what have we been missing?*

Footnote* There have been many
interesting results obtained from
experimenting with Infra and
Ultra-sound wavelengths as well.

Infrasonic waves are sound waves
that are lower in frequency than what
humans can hear. A subsonic wave is a
wave that is traveling slower than the
speed of sound and supersonic, or
ultrasonic waves travel faster.

In one such experiment
participants who were believed to be
"sensitive" or "intuitive" were placed
in the cells of an abandoned prison for
a period of time and asked if they felt
or sensed anything. Many of which
didn't claim to experience much at all.

They were then exposed to
infrasonic sound waves being emitted
from a speaker, just below the range of
human hearing. Surprisingly,
afterwards, many of the participants
claimed to experience deep feelings of
dread, depression and despair.

The Military is currently, and has
for some time been exploring and
experimenting with the psychoacoustic

effects of soundwaves on humans as well (the study of which leads to a whole host of afflictions and symptoms that the human organism can be subjected to due to exposure to different sound frequencies, including physiological disturbances).

For the purpose of employing non lethal force, especially in incidents where large crowds or groups of people need to be controlled at once, such as in occurrences of social unrest, like riots and unruly demonstrations or protests.

Shadow People

"I've heard of shadow people, and maybe even seen one. Are they a common entity?" ~question via email

One of the most interesting and intriguing phenomena in the world of paranormal activity is that of the "Shadow People." Each and every week there seems to be more and more stories and reports involving these mysterious beings, and they certainly have become a hot topic and a subject of growing interest in research by investigators.

Descriptions of these strange entities and their natures vary from harmless, quiet and shy observers, to malevolent and downright nasty creatures of mal-intent.

As with most things in the paranormal field, no one can say with any degree of certainty what these shadow beings are, but we will explore a few of the prevalent theories.

Shadow people have gained their nickname because they are most commonly observed or reported as having a human-like form. Unlike the typical descriptions of ghosts who are usually described as having human form with discernible characteristics such as physical features, clothing and accessories, shadow people are said to be feature-less humanoids.

Generally, they are described as appearing to have mass, though their natures seem to vary from simple two-dimensional shadows, to distorted three-dimensional forms.

Their movements are sometimes described as "unnatural," seeming to be very quick and disjointed. Sometimes they are said to move in slow motion, as if they were submerged in liquid, and then to suddenly move rapidly from one place to another within the room.

Again, some accounts differ even more widely and describe a completely black being with red eyes, a cloak, and a hat. This variation has come to be known as "the hat man."

Many witnesses describe feeling a strong presence or a sense of being watched, many times they will get a glimpse of 'something dark' out of the corner of their eye, they turn to look in the direction of the figure only to see it disappear into thin air, or flee right through a wall.

Sometimes they are reported as being childlike and playing games with witnesses. These seem to be curious and are also almost always seen through the periphery of vision. When the witness turns to look at them, rather than disappear through a wall or into thin air; they flee in a particular direction.

Once while spending some time alone at my house, my sister reported chasing a small child around from room to room. She said that as soon as she would enter one room, the child would disappear around the corner into another room. This went on for a few seconds and she said that it seemed as if it was a little boy, and he was playing with her.

About a week later we found out that my then significant other was pregnant, and she did end up giving birth to my first son.

Many times people interpret the presence of shadow people as being ominous and equate experiences with shadow beings with feelings of dread, ill intent and pure evil. Sometimes these shadow beings seem to be curious about the people who are seeing them. (which is a whole other interesting topic).

Various theories surrounding the nature and origin of shadow people abound. Some believe that they are inter-dimensional beings which exist in a universe parallel to our own. Others suggest that they are demonic entities, or are observers from another place.

Some even suggest that they may be thought forms unconsciously created by negative psychic energy and related to a place or event in which extreme emotional or physical stress/trauma has taken place.

It is extremely hard not to notice the subconscious symbolism implied by these manifestations. In Jungian Psychology and Philosophy the shadow is associated with the hidden aspects of the conscious mind; it is an archetype of the secret, repressed area of human nature and behavior, perhaps that is why feelings of fear and malevolence often accompany interaction with these beings.

Possible Scientific Explanations:

Hypnagogia

Some of the conditions reported in shadow people experiences are similar to occurrences in episodes of sleep paralysis. Oftentimes witnesses to shadow people have reported that the experiences occur just before falling asleep, or just after waking. Many times victims are in bed and report being 'held down' during visitations.

Physiologically, this could be the result of a condition called hypnagogic paralysis. The body naturally goes through a state of paralysis during REM sleep in order to keep us from acting out our dreams physically.

A temporary and unsettling paralysis can occur when we are suddenly awakened from an REM state into an awake state, but the bodily paralysis is still occurring. This causes the person to be fully aware, but unable to move.

In addition, in this state the person is sometimes able to consciously *perceive* images from their subconscious mind. These hallucinations can be very real and can include some, or all sensory perceptions; the individual can experience taste, smell, auditory, tactile, and/or visual phenomena.

Hypnagogia is sometimes known as 'the faces in the dark phenomenon' because sufferers commonly report seeing faces while experiencing waking-sleep. Similar hypotheses have been put forward linking this condition to a number of other apparent paranormal experiences, including alien abductions.

Pareidolia

In most instances, witnesses report seeing shadow people through their peripheral vision. This area of vision is linked to the area of the brain that is hard-wired to find familiar patterns, while providing less detail to the brain than center-forward vision does.

This can lead to a condition known as pareidolia, in which the brain incorrectly interprets random patterns of light/shadow or texture as being familiar patterns such as faces and human/animal forms, similar to seeing familiar shapes in clouds.

This phenomenon is known as 'matrixing' by many paranormal investigators.

Electromagnetic Fields

Recently, it has been found that electro-magnetic fields can interfere with the functions of the temporal lobe; creating altered states of perception in which auditory and visual hallucinations can occur.

In recent studies researchers have been able to recreate many of the experiences reported during paranormal encounters or hauntings under controlled conditions.

Similarly having also documented correlations between naturally-occurring magnetic fields and areas where paranormal events have been reported.

As I said in the opening of this article, there is no way to definitively explain any reported occurrences in the paranormal field -- yet.

However, if we are ever to get to the root of these matters, and be able to one day discover what the nature of these experiences are, it is important for us to keep records of personal experiences and for those who are experiencing these things to come forward, so that we can have these stories to contrast against findings in the field.

As for the shadow people, maybe they are a figment of our imaginations, maybe they are something more... Maybe they are the Gatekeepers, at The Crossroads.

The Sun and Paranormal Activity

It is believed that spirits manifest or exist within the vibrational frequencies on the IR end of the spectrum...

We all (should) know that the fields of Paranormal and Parapsychological research are still in their infancies. Therefore, most of what we believe to know about this subject is for the most part, theoretical.

To learn more we must continue to broaden our views and explore new concepts in trying to gain an understanding of what really may and may not be going on.

Keeping in tune with our article on Full Spectrum and UV Light in which we postulated that everything is composed of energy and vibration; Everything is said to vibrate at various frequencies. Spirits or ghosts are also assumed to be comprised of energy; and that energy may exist at vibrational rates higher or lower than our own.

This brought about a new angle of thought concerning the frequency and occurrences of observable paranormal activity. Namely, the time of day and regularity at which these phenomena are traditionally believed, and reported to take place.

In the past, I myself, when asked why paranormal occurrences seem to happen more at night have theorized things such as "perhaps our senses are heightened due to fear, or that there is less EMF interference from electrical equipment and appliances, etc..."

But now, with information about light, vibration, energy and frequencies being applied to our theories, we are forced to consider a new set of rules and probabilities.

As we said in the article on Full Spectrum Light, everything is made up of energy and vibrates at various rates, entities, spirits, ghosts may be more visible in other areas of the light spectrum than within the parameters of the very narrow range of light that makes itself available to human perception.

These different vibrational rates
are picked up and detected by our eyes
as colors. Higher numbers signify
longer wavelengths, which translate
into slower rates of vibration or
frequency, the lower the number, the
shorter the wave and higher the
frequency.

The lowest frequency of light we
can see appears as red to our eyes, and
the highest appears as violet, but as
we said, the entire spectrum of light
is much larger than this.

Most people do not realize how
important these various frequencies are
in our everyday lives.

In our past article we provided a
basic chart that demonstrated the light
spectrum as far as color and vibration
is concerned, but here we see the much
more further reaching implications of
the light spectrum and how these
various rates of vibration play a part
in our daily lives:

Directly below the infrared end of
the spectrum are microwaves followed by
the frequencies over which AM and FM
radio are broadcast, as well as cell
phones, CB and walkie-talkie radios,

satellite television and wireless internet connections.

It is believed that many spirits manifest or exist within the vibrational frequencies on the IR end of the spectrum… The UV and x-rays given off by the sun are known to not only disrupt the IR band, but it can fragment and scatter it!

The frequencies that most readily demonstrate this quality are AM and shortwave radio signals. That is why these bands are heard better at night and often signals can be picked up from distances hundreds of miles away, yet, in daylight, nothing but static is heard.

AM and short radio waves are more conductive, and 'skip' or 'bounce' off of the ionosphere at night, but they are scattered by the atmosphere in the daytime.

The rate, distance and time of this skip are determined by seasons, time of day, sunspots and solar flare activity; which can cause electrons to be released into the atmosphere that absorb lower frequency vibration and dampen conductivity within these bands.

Considering this, it seems reasonable to suggest that if spirits do indeed exist on higher and lower frequencies in the forms of energy, then perhaps their wavelengths can also be affected during day and night cycles.

Thus, it would be reasonable under these circumstances to assume that daylight and solar activity may very well be absorbing the energies required for "observable" paranormal activity to take place in some cases, if such instances are observable.

Buyer Beware

The research that lead to this article came from a friend who had contacted me to tell me that a friend of hers was in the process of buying a house, and the paperwork included a notice of disclosure that to the best of the current Home Owner's knowledge, the house was not haunted; and she was curious to know if I had ever heard of such a notice being included in the sale of a home.

Upon looking into the matter, I found that only certain states actually had disclosure laws in place where real estate is concerned. There are several physical and structural issues that could make a house undesirable such as old wiring, bad plumbing, a leaky roof or a compromised foundation, but what if there is something nonstructural that makes a house undesirable?

These are called "stigmatized properties" by Real Estate Professionals. As a matter of fact, in many states, an agent is prohibited from disclosing such information to a prospective buyer without the consent of the seller.

A stigmatized property is a home that can have a negative psychological impact on potential buyers or renters due to past events or situations that may have occurred there. These can include murders, suicides, criminal activity, Paranormal occurrences, the presence of cult members, and HIV or AIDS patients or a notorious previous owner living there.

In some cases, an entire family could have been murdered in a home prior to it being placed on the market, and the Real Estate Agent has zero obligation to inform prospective buyers of the house's history.

Stigmatized properties are defined as follows: "Any property that has no structural or foundational damages but other circumstances may make the property undesirable."

I came to discover that there was a case in upstate New York, in 1991, Stambovsky v.s. Ackley, in which the seller of a home in Nyack N.Y., Helen Ackley, owned a house which She had previously advertised to the public as being haunted by ghosts.

In 1989, Jeffery Stambovsky bought Helen Ackley's Victorian mansion for $650,000. Stambovsky, being a transplant from New York City, was unfamiliar with the house's reputation of being haunted.

Ackley had reported the existence of ghosts in the house to both Reader's Digest and a local newspaper on three occasions between 1977 and 1989, when the house was included on a five-home walking tour of the city.

Strombovsky bought the house without any knowledge that it was famously haunted with ghosts. When his new neighbors clued him in, Stambosky took the Ackleys to court to cancel the contract and get his money back. In the first trial, the judge denied Stambovsky's claim, citing *caveat emptor* or "let the buyer beware," But an appellate court in New York reversed the decision, ordering Ackley to return Stambovsky's money.

"Whether the source of the spectral apparitions seen by defendant seller are parapsychic or psychogenic, having reported their presence in both a national publication and the local press," wrote the court, "defendant is estopped [prevented from going back on her word] to deny their existence and, as a matter of law, the house is haunted."

The Court ultimately ruled that the haunted reputation of the house impacted both the value of the property and its resale potential. This however is a rare case, and if buyers want to know for sure if there are any pre existing circumstances that could deem a house as stigmatized, the burden is largely left upon the buyer to do their due diligence beyond a standard title search.

Unhealthy Infatuations

If you believe it, it is true to you, regardless of popular belief.

Recently, I was contacted by someone who claimed to be in possession of a few haunted dolls. She said that she had been collecting them for years, and that recently a couple of them started "acting up".

She claimed that, among other things, the dolls attacked her psychically in her dreams at night. I had to ask her, "What made you decide to start seeking out and collecting supposedly haunted dolls in the first place?" She never really gave me a direct answer, just that she had come across a few over the years and recently, she had been finding and buying them on Ebay and other such online sites.

This piqued my curiosity, and prompted me to look further into this area of interest. I went onto Ebay and to my surprise, there were 142 listings of "haunted dolls" available for sale, and 11,453 miscellaneous items that fell under the "Haunted" heading...

including everything from jewelry, dolls and vases, to spells and books!

On Craigslist, a similar listing contained the words "I will have a few real, Certified Haunted Dolls available for adoption from my personal collection."

Another Ebay merchant offered 'positive energy' blankets that "will comfort and protect your doll so that no dark energy will enter it." It goes on to say, "wrap your beloved up (in the blanket), so the positive and comforting energy can surround them and wrap them in a blanket of love."

Now, whether or not you or I believe in such things is not what is important here... what is important is that in many cases the individual who seeks out and buys these relics *does* believe that they are in fact haunted, which begs the question... why buy them?

I have at least one team associate who would assert that such things are possible, and they very well may be, but paranormal experiences seem to be, in most cases, closely related to personal belief.

So, if one believes that the souls of the deceased can inhabit an

inanimate object, such as a doll, and
one intentionally seeks out those items
and brings them into their home, then
wouldn't the resultant activity be par
for the course?

Further, wouldn't it be an
indication that you got exactly what
you wanted, and paid for?

From this standpoint, what anyone
else believes is irrelevant; if the
person being 'haunted' believes that
they are experiencing traumatizing
events, then who are we to say that
they are not?

As one who seeks to gather
information in the field of paranormal
studies, I sought (against my better
judgment) to at least interview the
haunted dolls client, to appease the
situation or put her mind at ease, we
set up a small investigation with
minimal equipment and a couple of group
members. A big part of what we do is to
help people, even if that entails a
couple of fruitless hours of
investigation.

In this particular case, we sent
two Team Members to the client's home.
We had her spread out the "problem
dolls" on her bed and we set up two EMF
(electro-magnetic frequency) meters
with the dolls, and put a video camera

near the foot of the bed to document any fluctuations in ambient energy fields that might occur.

Members then conducted a 2-hour EVP (electronic voice phenomena) session which entailed a series of generalized questions along with a few specific ones based on information provided by the client.

The client also provided us with a print out containing details about certain dolls in her collection, such as the names of previous owners and the circumstances surrounding how the doll supposedly came to be "haunted".

Prior to having them go out, I had met with the client and felt that there was nothing paranormal going on, besides an overactive imagination, but still it is our duty to follow up on leads as they come in.

As we had suspected, nothing was documented and there were no strange occurrences during our time with the client in the presence of her doll collection, but so it is with many investigative probes into these types of claims.

There is so little garnished from much of the hours spent on investigations, but that doesn't discourage us as researchers... One anomaly caught on video or audio makes up for the hours of seemingly wasted time spent at various locations at our own expenses.

As a society we are moving in a direction where more and more people are seeking answers, and in recent years television has certainly brought the paranormal field to the forefront of everyone's consciousness, but is this a healthy thing? I mean, this is what I do and love, but is it good for everyone?

Can any good come out of curious teens playing with Ouija Boards or holding impromptu séances? Is it conducive to progress in the field for thrill-seekers and would-be paranormal investigators to go out and buy a $20 digital audio recorder and attempt to conduct practice EVP sessions in their homes?

Could they potentially be opening up a door that they are not prepared or equipped to close? Are we not potentially opening the same doors and inviting the same energies and ideas into our lives and homes when we intentionally seek out objects with morbid histories attached to them?

Whether the door to the unknown is actual, spiritual or psychological, or a combination of all three, it is likely that the resulting effects will be very real to those who are susceptible to, and unwittingly open themselves up to these types of experiences.

With what we have learned thus far and from the documented information and accounts that are publicly available today, no one should unnecessarily endanger themselves or their loved ones by exposing them to an unknown force. No one should take such risks, and no one can claim that they had no idea of what could potentially happen; there are just too many examples to draw from.

The energies involved can be volatile in many cases, and curious thrill seekers may be getting more than they bargained for when they collect things or engage in activities that may attract ethereal beings. Be smart and be safe.

Recurrent Spontaneous Psychokinesis
RSPK

Recurrent Spontaneous Psychokinesis is poltergeist-like activity that causes disturbances in the environment while a person (called the Agent) is present. It was once believed that poltergeists were entities in their own right, but recent research suggests that it is actually the result of the unconscious mind of the Agent.

This is typically exemplified by the movement of household items such as furniture and fixtures in the immediate vicinity of said Agent.

It has been observed that the vast majority of these cases involve a child or teenager, usually pubescent in age, and in particular, female. It is believed that this is the result of the many changes females go through (hormonal and psychological) during this time period. Emotional stress and turmoil coupled with fluctuating hormone levels are externalized into the surrounding environment causing physical disturbances, or unconscious psychokinesis.

This would work in similar fashion as telekinesis, where one can seemingly move objects at will with their mind, but is instead involuntary.

This was observed in the case of one Eleonore Zogun in 1913. Activity surrounding Eleonore started three months before her 12th birthday. Items began moving in her house and rocks were being thrown outside. This continued for two years and ended abruptly after she began her very first menstrual cycle.

There have yet been other studies that have linked cases of RSPK to symptoms of Complex Partial Seizures or CPS. One study conducted by the Epilepsy Foundation found that in very rare cases, during the onset of puberty in adolescent females, that there was an increase in CPS activity which could also lead to RSPK activity.

In another nother instance, known as the Rosenheim Poltergeist, the activity was centred around a young woman named Annemarie Schneider in Rosenheim, Bavaria. She was a secretary in the law office of Sigmund Adam. Annemarie seemed to be the cause of strange activity in the office. Lights would turn off and on, drawers on desks would open and close seemingly on their own, pictures turned upside down on their hooks and telephones would ring without anyone calling.

A Parapsychologist named Hans Bender was called to investigate the occurrences and he noticed that when Annemarie was present, so was the activity. When she was away from the office, or on vacation, the activity stopped. He determined that Annemarie herself was likely the source of the activity. After interviewing her, he discovered that she had just experienced some type of "serious personal relationship trauma" which likely triggered the activity.

Another researcher, W.G. Roll, suggested a link between epilepsy and poltergeist activity. He said that he found that 22 out of 92 persons regarded as the center of such activity he had surveyed were prone to "seizures or dissociative states" In one particularly noteworthy case (Solfvin & Roll, 1976), poltergeist-like eruptions appeared to alternate with seizures in a grand mal epileptic patient.

Though it seems most common for a female to be at the center of this phenomenon, It can also have a male agent as I will demonstrate: We had a case a few years back where we were contacted by a man who claimed that he was experiencing all types of disturbances in his home.

He claimed that the radio would sometimes turn itself off or on, and anytime he would tune in to the local Christian station, the radio would fall violently off of the kitchen counter as if thrown. Landing feet away in the middle of the kitchen floor. He also claimed that on at least one occasion, he saw a very large hand draw his kitchen curtain open while he was in the backyard cutting the grass.

During our interview he told me that he was ex military and had been stationed in Korea where he met his wife, and brought her to the United States. After some time together she requested that he set aside one of the rooms in their house for her to have as a shrine room to worship and meditate in. Which he did.

It was about this time, or soon thereafter, that he began experiencing strange things in the house. Especially when alone. Being raised as a devout catholic he had been condemned by his own conscience for allowing the space in his house. This was an externalization of his own inner turmoil or guilt associated with feeling as if he had transgressed or compromised his own religious beliefs to please his wife.

All of this is just to say that we still do not understand the nature of paranormal activity. It may very well be the result of our own minds, as can be observed in the case of hauntings and obsessions. The more we are made aware of something, the stronger it gets. Someone was just telling me that they grew up with a haunted slave doll in their home that had been passed down through the last few generations.

Everyone had to acknowledge the doll upon entering the room or "something bad would happen." They had effectively created an egregore. When everyone in the home starts talking about the entity, acknowledging it, it feeds on the energy being given to it.

What is the Weight of the Human Soul?

Can one measure the weight of the flame, or the mass of the human soul?

It had been used as a philosophical and Theological paradox for centuries, aimed mainly at those who took a scientific approach to find answers to the universe's mysteries to show them that not all things were knowable.

Tauntingly demonstrating that while some may have disputed the existence of the soul because it cannot be measured in weight or mass, yet a flame is observable and few would repute the reality of its existence in spite of the inability to weigh its mass.

In the early twentieth century, one Dr. Duncan MacDougall seems to have set out to tackle this enigma head on.

On April 10, 1901, Dr. MacDougall began conducting experiments in Dorchester, Massachusetts. Dr. MacDougall had determined to prove that the human soul both had *mass*, and was *measurable* in weight. He conducted this experiment on six dying patients who were placed on scales just prior to their times of death.

What he intended to do was to weigh each person before, during and after death to determine if there was any measurable difference detected on the scales. The patients were carefully selected based upon the likelihood of imminent death. Two patients were suffering from tuberculosis, five are reported to have been men and one was a woman.

When it was determined that death was only a few hours away MacDougall would have the entire bed placed on an industrial sized scale which was set to measure by the gram. With four other Doctors present and observing his experiment, Dr. MacDougall measured the weight of his first patient prior to his death.

Once the patient died, a remarkable observation had been recorded; "Suddenly, coincident with death," wrote MacDougall, "The beam end dropped with an audible stroke hitting against the lower limiting bar and remaining there with no rebound. The loss was ascertained to be three-fourths of an ounce."

The experiment continued on the next patient with similar findings. A quote about the experiments in an article from the March 11, 1907 edition of the New York Times read:

"The instant life ceased, the opposite scale pan fell with a suddenness that was astonishing - as if something had been suddenly lifted from the body. Immediately all the usual deductions were made for physical loss of weight, and it was discovered that there was still a full ounce of weight unaccounted for."

While not all the subjects of the experiment lost the same amount of weight, they did all lose a measurable amount that could not be explained or accounted for. Everything was taken into account, from the air in the lungs to bodily fluids, yet the weight loss still could not be explained.

At the completion of his study he found that his results supported his original hypothesis, that the human soul indeed had mass. Further, he concluded that when the soul departed from the body, so did this mass.

Based on taking an average of the total weight lost by his subjects, and taking into account the notes and measurements taken by the other doctors present during his experiment, Dr.

MacDougall determined that the soul weighed roughly 21 grams.

Other studies were carried out to confirm the results. Experiments on mice and other animals took place.

Dr. MacDougall also conducted the same experiment on 15 dogs. The experiments showed no change in weight following their death. MacDougall concluded this to signify only humans have souls which supports my personal theory about the nature, origin and final destination of the soul but you'll have to do further research for yourselves on this topic if you're interested in finding out more about that…

Again, in 1988 a group of East German Researchers conducted the same experiment on over 200 terminally ill subjects.

Same as before, the subjects were weighed before, during and after death. In this study, the weight loss with each patient was exactly the same, time after time: $1/3000^{th}$ of an ounce.

Could this difference in weight be due to the use of more precise and sensitive scales in 1988 in comparison to those available to Dr. MacDougall in 1901?

Or, are we diminishing spiritually as we learn to depend and rely more and more on science, technology as 'facts'?

Fallen Angels, Aliens, and Giants

Sumer was the first advanced civilization of human beings on Earth, long ahead of the famed dynasties of Egypt.

Recently, I watched the movie *The Fourth Kind*. While I found the film to be thoroughly entertaining, I immediately knew that the producers claims that the film was based on factual events containing footage from actual hypnosis sessions involving the victims and their therapist were *false*.

In spite of that, what I did enjoy was the fact that the filmmakers touched on a subject that is of great interest to me, but perhaps not commonly familiar among the vast majority of the population.

In the film, some of the residents of a small town in Alaska seem to be having trouble sleeping. They end up seeing a local psychologist who utilizes hypnotherapy to get them to recall the source of their night terrors.

While under hypnosis it is revealed that the patients are being visited and abducted by alien visitors who seem to be subjecting them to a battery of scientific and physiological examinations.

Nothing new or original there, but an interesting turn comes about when a non-human voice is recorded in the psychologist's house. The voice is speaking in a strange language (as aliens probably would) that is later realized to be Sumerian.

At one point in the film, one of the extra terrestrial beings is heard in a recording making references to "our creation" and also stating "I am God."

This is when I really started paying attention because this plays into a couple of theological ideas surrounding UFO's and the nature of the beings that pilot them. Currently, more people are probably familiar with the idea that extraterrestrials or "aliens" are believed by some to be angelic or demonic beings that are related to the Bible's account in Genesis 6 of "Giants" or Nephilim (Fallen Ones) or Annunaki as they are know in the Sumerian mythos.

A little background: The ancient civilization of Sumer was located in the region now known as Iraq, and was situated between the Euphrates and the Tigris rivers, an area known as Mesopotamia or the cradle of civilization.

Sumer is believed to be the first advanced civilization of human beings on Earth. Their kingdom flourished about 6000 years ago, well before the dynasties of Ancient Egypt.

The Sumerians were the first to develop a system of writing and record keeping, they had developed an advanced form of mathematics which allowed them to divide into fractions and decimals, and they were also the first to develop a calendar, and were notably keen throughout the region in the area of astronomy.

They drew a model of our solar system with the sun at its center, a fact not known to European or modern scientists until about 300 years ago. They had the first cities and urban planning boards; they had schools which taught language and writing, as well as the sciences of the day such as botany, zoology, geography, mathematics, and theology. Literary works were also studied and composed.

There is even evidence that they possessed a rather sophisticated form of technology. What many scholars and scientists believe to be early battery cells have been found throughout the region, they are known as Baghdad batteries and are at least 2300 years old.

Though they were polytheists, the Sumerians had a rather complex religious system in place, much of which parallels Egyptian and Hebraic religion.

Anyone who has conducted a reasonable amount of study into the religious writings of ancient civilizations would say that it is fair to assert that the Sumerian writings had a great deal of influence on the beliefs of subsequent cultures that emerged from that region.

It is also to be noted that the family of the Patriarch Abraham of the Bible originated from the Land of Ur, which was a city-state of ancient Sumer.

In fact, the oldest telling of the Deluge, or flood story comes from a Sumerian text known as the Eridu Genesis. In it, the gods decide to destroy humanity for their defiance, but Enki (the god of wisdom) secretly warns a man named Ziusudra, instructing him to build a huge ark and to take mating pairs of animals into it so that the earth may be repopulated after the flood is over.

Another similarity between the Sumerian and Hebrew scriptures comes in Genesis 6, where we see that the "fallen ones" or angels that have rebelled against God, come to earth and procreate with human women creating a race of hybrid, half human, half angelic beings.

These are known as The Nephilim or Napal (fallen ones) in Hebrew. It was because of this mixing that the Biblical account of the story tells us that God decides to destroy humanity, because they have become tainted with angelic "genes."

Only Noah was found to be "Perfect in his generations," or untainted and of pure blood.

In the Sumerian text, there is also a race of beings that come from the skies, they are known as the Anunnaki which translates as "those who came down from the heavens."

According to the Sumerian mythos, the Anunnaki, being highly technologically advanced, spliced their DNA into the genes of Homo Erectus, producing Homo Sapiens to be their servants.

The Sumerians were great at keeping records, excavations of the ancient site shed light on the amazingly advanced civilization of Sumer and with it, thousands of clay tablets containing not only public records of commerce, marriages and military actions, but also advanced astronomical calculation systems and of the written history of the Anunnaki themselves!

It is apparent from detail in those records that the Sumerians believed that the offspring of these aliens were real flesh and blood members of their society.

One of the most impressive finds was a sealed nine foot by six foot room in Sippar holding a set of 400 clay tablets containing an unbroken record of the history of those times neatly arranged on shelves. Like a sort of time capsule.

The recovered records place the location of the Anunnaki laboratory where the first humans were literally produced in east central Africa in the same location on the map where the mitochondrial DNA "search for Eve" places the first woman Homo Sapiens and in the same time-period.

The writings also include detailed descriptions of our solar system matching what we now know and beyond. It describes the orbit of a tenth planet between Mars and Jupiter. They say that this planet, called Niburu (which means the planet of crossing) was thrust into our solar system and collided with a planet called Tiamat.

The remaining bulk of Tiamat became Eridu or the Earth, and the fragments that were left became the asteroid belt (how could they possibly know about the existence of an asteroid belt?).

Niburu took orbit in retrograde, in an elongated orbit around our sun and passes between mars and Jupiter approximately every 3600 years.

According to the texts, this information was given to the Sumerians by the Anunnaki, who came from the planet Nibiru. It is believed by some that this information prompted scientists to search for the unknown planet that they refer to as planet X.

This also ties in with 2012 theories, some believe that 2012 actually marks the approximate time that Nibiru would cross through our solar system again, an event that would cause many anomalies in the earth, as the planet likely has its own magnetic poles and gravitational pull which could interfere with those of the earth, causing natural disasters.

Another interesting note is that throughout *The Fourth Kind*, the arrival of the beings is somehow connected to the appearance of an owl outside of the witnesses' homes. The Sumerian deity Moloch was oftentimes depicted as an owl and is named as one of the greatest warriors from among the fallen in John Milton's Paradise lost.

Whether these similarities are coincidental, or the result of my own overactive imagination making connections where none are, possibly a side effect of too much study, only the film writers and producers can say, but what about you? Do you believe in the possibility of the existence of extraterrestrial beings?

What of the Sumerians? How did they learn about our universe and solar

system without the use of a telescope?
And how were they able to draw detailed
and precise maps which depicted the
position and sizes of the various
planets in relation to one another?

Is it possible that they were
visited by interplanetary beings who
taught them these sciences? If so, what
does that mean for us today?

If there are such beings, do they
mean harm to us harm, or are they just
examining us the same way that we
examine wildlife?

Abducting them out of their natural
habitations and dwellings and
inspecting and tagging them, releasing
them back into the wild with implants
and identifying marks that help us
track them and monitor their migration
and mating patterns.

Makes you wonder...

Bump In The Night

"I've heard that paranormal activity is highest at night. Why would this be?" ~question via email

I believe we are either brought up with, or somehow develop a natural association with fear and darkness. A pitch-black room or sitting around a campfire at night are the perfect settings in which to share ghost stories and scare our friends, *let's face it*, in the dark we are more susceptible to our imaginations!

The concrete lines of what "is" and "is not" become softened and the two worlds ooze into one another, we are no longer as confident about what may and may not be lurking in the unseen as we are in the light.

To expect that paranormal or ghostly activity occurs mainly at night has more to do with this same brand of fear than anything else. Not saying that paranormal activity does not occur at night, but in my estimation, if it is indeed a reality, it should not be regulated to any particular time of day, though it is possible that certain occurrences are more easily observable under these conditions.

Most accounts of paranormal activity that have been brought to my attention have actually occurred during daylight hours or at least while the lights were turned on at the location. Believing that "ghosts" or entities are only active at night is akin to believing that the stars are only in the sky at night.

There are, however, at least a couple of theories floating around among Paranormal Investigators as to why activity may be more likely to occur at night than during waking hours. Some theorize that we are more apt to notice things during night hours due to a heightening of our other senses brought on by being deprived of the faculty of sight.

Other investigators speculate that 3:00 a.m. is "the demonic hour" because it is an inversion of 3:00 p.m., which is believed to be the hour of Jesus' death. According to this train of thought, 3:00 a.m. would be used by demons as the hour to mock his death... and 12:00 midnight is known as the witching hour.

From a psychological point of view, I think it is fair to say that at night, in the dark, we are more prone to attribute a sound or a movement to something paranormal because of fear. We instinctively fear what we do not know or understand... and darkness is, in the symbolic language of the human subconscious, the embodiment of ALL that is unknown.

According to popular opinion, a good reason for conducting paranormal investigations in total darkness is to be able to turn off all power in an area to better observe fluctuations in EMF fields, and while on the surface this may seem to be a reasonable technique, it has serious drawbacks. Aside from picking up changes in an immediate, localized area, EMF meters also pick up fluctuations in the earth's magnetic fields and can detect lightning from as much as 6 miles away!

In the case of televised paranormal investigation, conducting every investigation in total darkness is for little more than dramatic effect because one could just as readily create a power-free environment during daylight hours by simply flipping the main power switch inside a location.

Paranormal activity is unpredictable for the most part, and who is to say that in the otherworldly realm (that our ghostly neighbors inhabit) night and day even exist?

Perhaps being afraid of the dark acts as a catalyst of some sort, the fear or uncertainty primes our minds, enabling us to catch a glimpse of something or have an experience that we otherwise would have been shut off to…

Our minds filter incoming information from our environments based on what we expect and accept as normal. The brain disregards some bits of information while it can also completely fabricate others to coincide with our expectations of what reality is (or is not). The darkness embraces and encloses us in its ambiguous arms, totally engulfing us while concealing from our view everything around us.

The bottom line I believe is this, whether or not specters and spooks are among us in the daylight... we all fear the things... that go bump in the night.

Introduction to Ghost Stories

The following section is a short compilation of accounts that have been shared with me over the years by the people who experienced them.

They are all purported to be TRUE accounts of the events as they took place. I have changed the names unless granted express permission by the recounter.

As you can probably imagine, I have collected quite a few stories over the years, but the ones I have chosen to share here are the ones that were either the most interesting to me, or that seemed to have had the most impact on those who had the experiences.

Do you have a ghost story that you would like to share? Maybe a tale that has been passed down by a family member? Feel free to contact me via the email form on bernardpowell.com.

You can also upload images and videos you may have of anomalous activity, beings or artifacts.

A Ghost in Residence

This is a true story, as far as I know...
Only the names of those involved have been changed since I am retelling their story, as it was told me:

Mary and her husband Jim were the parents of three young children, 9 year old Becky, 6 year old Sara, and the youngest, James Jr. who was 2 at the time. They lived very modestly in a small 2-bedroom apartment in a building situated on a bad block in a rough part of town.

Through the years, Mary and Jim had not been able to establish good enough credit to buy a house, but they had been saving money here and there in hopes of one day moving to a home in a safer neighborhood.

When a rash of shootings and burglaries broke out in the area Mary and Jim decided it was time to make a drastic change for their children's safety no matter what the price.

They began looking at homes available for rent in the city's upper middle class north end, the rent was high but the schools were much better and the streets were quiet and lined with Victorian style homes with neatly manicured lawns and white picket fences, very different from the noisy garbage littered streets from which they came.

After some time they found a home within their price range. Though the moving costs wiped out most of their savings, but at least they would be able to sleep in peace knowing that their family was safe.

The house in the suburbs was quite large and beautiful, hardwood flooring and decorative wallpaper complimented the intricate trim detail and crown moldings. Yet there seemed to be something else going on beneath the surface.

It wasn't long before Mary started to notice that something was strange about their new home, whenever she was alone in the house she often felt as if she was being watched... sometimes she thought she caught glimpses of "shadows" darting across the room out of the corner of her eye.

She dismissed the experiences and chalked it up to being in such a large quiet space. All her life she had lived in apartment buildings with neighbors living above, beneath, and sometimes to either sides of her, she had never really experienced such tranquility and quiet like this before. *That had to have been it;* her mind was simply playing tricks on her.

One Autumn day Mary was at home doing housework and she started to experience the sensation of being watched again. She paused and glanced around the room not to merely catch a fleeting glimpse of something out of the corner of her eye, but a man! He was short and dark skinned, apparently of Latino descent.

He was standing in the doorway that led into the dining room, leaning against the frame with his hands in his pockets. He wore a pale yellow polo-style shirt with blue jeans and a baseball cap, and he was smiling a tight-lipped smile, and shaking his head from side to side.

He looked as if he had been standing there waiting for her to see him! As soon as she looked at him, he turned and walked out of sight, into the dining room.

Mary dropped the vacuum cleaner and instinctively chased after him. As she entered the dining room she caught only a brief glance of him rounding the corner into the kitchen. Entering the kitchen she caught sight of him rounding the corner into the laundry room, then down to the basement.

Frightened, she ran back into the living room, grabbed her shoes, jacket and car keys, and left the house until Jim came home. He checked the entire house and assured her that no one else was there.

A couple of months went by without any major incidents and Mary began to doubt what she thought she had seen that day, maybe Jim was right after all, maybe she was just exhausted and fatigued from worrying about their finances and working as much overtime as she could to help make ends meet.

Then, as Christmas was approaching, Mary began to see the shadows again.

Jim was outside one night helping an elderly neighbor set up Christmas lights on a tree in his front yard when the man casually said, "I'm surprised you guys have stayed there for so long, I don't usually have time to get acquainted with people who move into that house because they don't stay very long."

Jim asked him what he meant and he said, "A worker died in that house about 8 years ago, they say he never left. Everyone who has moved in there since has been spooked by something, and then they move."

Jim dared not tell Mary about this, it would only fuel her fears, and he asked their neighbor not to mention it to her either, nor would he tell her that HE had started having strange experiences and feelings in the home recently, especially at night, in the kitchen.

Christmas was beautiful in their new home, though they did not have much, they had each other. Family, friends and co-workers contributed towards buying gifts for their children that year, though despite the festivities they both could sense a lingering presence that seemed to constantly be nearby... watching.

By this time, friends and relatives began to complain about feeling an uneasiness and sense of being unwelcomed in their new home. It seemed as if things were getting progressively worse.

Taking the advice of a friend Mary decided that she should have the home *cleansed*, so she contacted an interfaith Minister that her friend recommended to her.

After a preliminary walk around, the Minister agreed something was going on in their home and he performed an impromptu house blessing but informed her that it could take several attempts before the spirit actually left the home and "crossed over."

That night, the activity levels in the house reached an all time high for Mary and her family. As soon as everyone was home strange noises began to come from the basement. Mary had not gone down there since her first experience with the dark skinned man.

It seemed as if things were falling or being thrown around down there. Then, they heard a loud crash *upstairs*, as if something almost came through the ceiling!

Jim bolted to the top of the landing to find that the tall chest-of-drawers in their bedroom had been knocked down! It lay face down on the floor and the clock radio and items that were on top were scattered about the room.

Jim said that he then felt a hand on his shoulder, but he knew that he was upstairs alone. He dashed out of the room and down the stairs without looking back.

By this time the baby was crying and the older children were clearly upset and afraid, everything had spiraled out of control into total chaos!

Mary and Jim decided to leave the house, at least for the night. In a panic and rushed fervor they clumsily fumbled with the children, trying to get their shoes and coats together to get them out to the car, but there was one problem... it was freezing outside and they couldn't find little Jim's coat. All he was wearing was a t-shirt and underwear.

Mary ran upstairs into little Jim's bedroom and standing there in the middle of the room was the same man she had seen before.

She let out a startled scream and Jim came running up to see what had happened. Mary could tell from his expression that he had seen the man too, standing there smiling, this time with his teeth showing, unusually long and discolored.

Not fangs mind you; he just had abnormally long brownish yellow colored teeth.

He was wearing the same baseball cap and pale yellow polo shirt Mary had seen him in before but there was something different this time... He was WEARING little Jim's coat!

The cuffs of the sleeves were just barely past the middle of his upper arms and the bottom of the dark blue coat hung just a few inches below his armpits. Mary and Jim nearly tripped over each other trying to get back downstairs.

They grabbed the children as they were and rushed them out the door and into the car, screeched out of the driveway and sought refuge at a relatives home.

The next morning Jim and his brother-in-law went back to the house to gather some of their belongings, Mary had already told him that she was never going back there under any circumstances.

When they walked in the front door, the first thing to catch Jim's eye was his son's dark blue coat sitting as if neatly laid out, in the middle of the living room floor.

Mary never did go back to the house. They left most of their belongings there and had to start all over, in a neighborhood similar to where they had started off...

I guess living in the suburbs isn't always all it's cracked up to be.

Baby in the Woods

It was a hot summer day in North Carolina. Just over 100 degrees and there wasn't very much shade on the land surrounding their grandparents secluded home.

For as long as they could remember, Tanya and her brother had come to the South to spend their summer vacations on their Grandparent's farm. Their grandma and grandpa lived on a 15 acre farm that they worked all by themselves, and during the summer months, Tanya and her older brother Greg left the noise and bustle of the big city behind and spent time on the farm with their grandparents, helping them prepare for the harvest that followed the summer months.

Things were so different here, it felt as if they were worlds away. In the city there was always noise and people around, here in the country there were different sounds, but for the most part it was quiet.

Especially at night.

At home during vacations they

stayed in bed as long as they wanted; but here, not only were they expected to wake up early, but both of them had a list of chores that needed to be done by lunchtime every day.

There was a heavily wooded area just on the outskirts of the farm. Their grandma and grandpa didn't like for them to venture too far off of the farm itself, into the woods.

At night it seemed as if strange sounds came out of the woods, "animals probably" Greg always assured Tanya, "That's all that could be out there, probably just stray dogs." But Tanya wasn't so sure...

One day after their chores were done, they were running off to go explore the property, "Don't y'all go past the fields!" their grandma yelled, "We won't!" they shouted back as they disappeared into the cornfield...

As they neared the woods Tanya heard a baby crying in the distance; "Shhh, Greg listen… Do you hear that?" "Yeah," he said. "I hear it. Sounds like a baby crying. They told us to stay away from the woods, maybe there are PEOPLE living out there. Maybe they're DANGEROUS! We should get back to the house and tell them that we..."

"NO!" Tanya said sharply, cutting her brother off mid sentence, "they'll be angry! They told us to stay away from the woods."
"OK." he agreed.

About a week had passed and they were starting to think that maybe they had mistaken what they had heard that afternoon. Maybe there was a farm with animals on it just past the woods. "Maybe we just heard sheep," Greg had convinced himself.

A few days later, while riding on the tractor with her brother, a good distance away from the house, Tanya heard something familiar, closer to the house this time; the faint sound of a baby crying!

It seemed to be coming from the field just ahead of them. She told her brother to stop the tractor. He did. She jumped out and cautiously made her way through the knee high grass, the sound of the distressed child seemed to be getting louder, and nearer.

Soon she came to an area where the grass seemed to have been trodden down and flattened; and laying right in the center of it, was an infant wrapped in an old dirty burlap cover.

She looked around and could not see anyone who could have put the baby there. She called over to her brother, "Greg!"

He walked over and stared in disbelief. "It WAS a baby we had heard that day" He thought to himself. "What should we do?" Tanya asked. "Leave it" Jim suggested; "I'm sure someone wouldn't just leave their baby laying in a field."
"We can't." Tanya picked the infant up and they began to make their way back towards the tractor. "Hurry up, we have to get back to the house to show grandma and grandpa what we found."

The child never stopped crying. Tanya laid the baby in her lap as her brother made his way through the field towards the house. Her mind was reeling. She wasn't paying much attention to the baby in her lap, she was glancing around, expecting to see someone chasing after them, wanting their baby back.

Her thoughts began to wander, she was wondering how her grandparents would react to her story. Her body was relaxed, she noticed how her head and neck were being tossed side to side and bounced around with the movement of the tractor riding across the bumps and dips of the field.

That's when she noticed something was wrong.

She snapped out of her daydream to realize that the baby had stopped crying and somehow it seemed to be getting heavier in her lap. it was… growing!

She looked down and saw that the child's features were beginning to distort and grow disproportionately. The eyes and mouth were abnormally large, and it looked as if teeth were in its mouth and the burlap sack looked as if it could hardly contain the child's body which now seemed to be twisted and contorted to fit into the bag.

The cries had turned into a deep gurgling sound and Tanya was frozen in terror! Her brother looked down at the baby and screamed. That's when things really began to get strange! A deep guttural voice came out of the child. He said "Put Me Baaack!"

They both left the tractor with the baby in it and ran back to the house as fast as they could. They burst through the kitchen door and both began trying to tell their Grandma what had happened at the same time:
"We were in the tractor and heard the baby from the people in the woods crying and..."

"The baby started turning into a monster..."
"I told her we shouldn't have gone into the woods..."

Their grandmother called grandpa into the kitchen and relayed the story to him. "Come out and show me where" he said. "I'm not going back out there" Tanya said.

"You have to. You're the one who moved him, you're going to have to put him back, or he'll find his way to the house tonight to find you since I'm sure you didn't walk backwards to the house."

As they found their way back to the tractor, Tanya's grandfather told her that he had an experience with the baby years before.

He said that the baby was what is known as a jumbee, the spirit of a child conceived during a forbidden union, whose mother hid her pregnancy and had gone into the woods to give birth to the child secretly.

She had intended to drown the child in a nearby brook, but she died during childbirth, leaving the living child alone to die of starvation. His earthbound soul cries for his mother to devour her when she finds him.

As they approached the tractor, they could hear the terrifying cries coming from the horribly disfigured lump of flesh that lay on the floor of the truck, screaming and writhing as if in pain.

Tanya's grandpa pulled a bag of

salt out of his pocket and made a line dividing the back of the tractor, from the front. "If he's able to drag himself along the floor, he won't be able to cross that line. Get in!"

They climbed into the tractor and her grandpa turned the wheel as she pointed him in the direction where they found the baby.

He hit the gas pedal and headed towards the edge of the property. "Right over there?"
"Yes, in that part of the field." Tanya looked back and it seemed as if almost immediately the twisted form began to change back.

It started to shrink and through the shadows it looked as if the head and face were once again starting to look like those of an infant. It got smaller and smaller until at last... it began to cry again as a newborn baby.

"Hurry, pick him up and put him back where you found him, it'll be dark soon!"

"Oh," he interjected, as if he had just remembered something important;

"and walk back to the tractor backwards!"

"But why..."

"Just DO IT Tanya!"

"Ok..."

She could see the patch of flattened grass ahead of her where she found the baby. It would be getting dark soon and she didn't want to be outside when the sun went down.

She hurried to the spot and quickly laid the baby down and started to run back to her grandfather waiting in the tractor, Oh wait! She remembered, walking backwards.

She didn't understand why, but none of this made any sense to her at this point. She turned and faced the baby on the ground and began to walk backwards to the tractor.

She climbed in backwards and began to position herself to sit in the seat. She hadn't sat down completely when her grandfather hit the gas pedal, knocking her into the seat.

Her grandfather was quiet considering everything that had just happened.

"I told you kids to stay away from the woods" he finally said, breaking the silence between them. "Why didn't you just tell us the reason why? You could have just told us the truth about the woods and the baby."

" Would you have believed me if I did?"
Tanya was silent.
"Sometimes you kids just need to listen and trust that their parents and grandparents know what's best!"

Out of Bounds

Frances and Emma Johnson were an elderly couple that lived in a quaint country style home in the *now* urban neighborhood in the town where I grew up.

They were considered to be pretty mean and unfriendly towards children as far as the neighborhood kids were concerned. Whenever children were playing nearby, if their the ball would go into the Johnson's yard you might as well consider it *gone*.

Let me explain:

Once, my friend Richard climbed their fence and ran across the back yard to retrieve a tennis ball that we had been playing with, and he was pelted with chestnuts that old lady Emma Johnson had gathered from the trees on her property.

She kept a large bowl of these chestnuts near her back door for this very purpose, she would come out onto her back porch and fire off a seemingly never ending barrage of chestnuts at any kid who dared to venture onto her property.

It was customary when a new kid moved into the neighborhood and was playing with the regulars, to make him go to the Johnson's front door and ring their doorbell, asking if he could go into their back yard to retrieve the ball.

Of course he would quickly see that this was a grave mistake, Emma would throw open her front door screaming at him to get his delinquent back-side off of her porch and not to set foot on her property ever again.

"I, I just wanted to know if it was ok to go into your backyard to get our ball," the new kid would plead coyly only to be met with more of the same type of response: "Anything on my property belongs to me!" Emma would bark; "Stay the hell out of my yard, or you'll be sorry!"

The other kids would all laugh and run across the street and so was the established relationship between the Johnson's and every kid in the neighborhood.

It was also like a rite of passage to jump their fence and try to retrieve the ball without permission, since it seemed to always end up in their backyard, and save the day.

The neighborhood kids weren't the only people who Emma seemed to take every opportunity to fight with, her husband was seldom seen with a smile on his face, and the two of them arguing was a common sound on Saturday mornings when the local kids would be meeting up in the empty lot across the street from their home.

The Johnson's bickered incessantly. In the driveway when they returned from the grocery store, coming out the front door on Sunday mornings on their way to church, out of the car and back into the house after returning from church... it was endless!

We all wondered how old man Johnson did it. We jokingly used to say that he probably couldn't wait to die; it would be a much-needed break from her!

Well, one winter morning old man Johnson suffered a heart attack and died in his front yard while shoveling snow from his porch, and down the walkway to the driveway.

It was strange for the neighborhood kids knowing he was gone, and out of some type of respect we stopped jumping the Johnson's fence for a period of time, like there was some kind of an unspoken peace treaty in effect.

Mrs. Johnson never eased up though; she was still as hard on us as ever, but not for long. About 8 months after Mr. Johnson had passed, so did Emma. Some people said she died of loneliness, others that she just missed having someone to yell at.

The house stood empty, a creepy testament to the horrible woman who had once lived there. The grass and bushes that Emma took so much pride in while she was alive were all overgrown and overtaken by weeds and wild shrubs, the lawn was brown and dusty and the screen door on the front porch was not completely closed so it would swing and sway with the breeze, making a creaking sound as it moved back and forth on windy days.

It was a dark night on Halloween that year, when a group of the neighborhood kids had been out trick or treating and had gathered in the empty lot to look over their loot and compare bags.

They were so engrossed in trying to see what each other had gotten and who had the most candy that they almost didn't notice what was happening in the background. It seemed so natural, so commonplace.

"WAIT! Does anyone else hear that?" One of the kids yelled out over the voices of the others. They all looked at one another as a sinking feeling went through the group.

Was that the sound of voices? Were those voices coming out of the Old Johnson house? Those were not just any voices... they all turned their attention to the house across the street, it sounded like the voices of Emma and Frances Johnson, and it sounded like they were arguing inside of the house *that stood in total darkness!*

They all heard it, historically when the couple was alive Halloween was a night unlike all others, the Johnson's reputation was such that no one ever rang their doorbell, or went to their house on Halloween.

The house had always remained with the lights off at night. There was definitely something going on across the street at the old house, but no one wanted to go check it out.

The next day, to their surprise when the kids gathered outside, there were dozens of balls scattered throughout the front yard of the old house. Tennis balls, baseballs, playground balls, footballs, basketballs and soccer balls thrown all about the yard and driveway.

It looked like the old lady had never thrown any of them away. Did someone break in there last night? Is that what they had heard? That must have been it, I mean, what else could it have been? Mr. and Mrs. Johnson arguing from beyond the grave? Of course not! How silly of them to think so, even for a moment!

The kids got together and gathered all the balls out of the front yard, yet somehow they still felt unwelcomed, as if they were not supposed to be there.

Even with the Johnson's gone it felt as if there was an unseen presence watching. Feeling the discomfort, they just collected as many balls as they could carry out of the yard and spent the rest of the afternoon playing and having a great time.

Then the inevitable happened... Someone kicked the ball and it soared overhead, it went back, back, back, over the fence and bounced up the driveway and into the backyard of the old house.

Enjoying his newfound sense of liberty, one of the kids decided he was going to go ahead and walk through the front gate, up the driveway and into the backyard to get the ball back. After all, what was stopping him?

The other kids cheered him on, semi tauntingly. As he opened the front gate he could feel an enormous amount of pressure, it seemed as if he could feel the eyes of everyone on his back, watching him enter the yard and waiting for him to retreat in fear.

The grass was pretty high in the backyard, high enough that he could not easily spot the ball. He had to walk into the yard a bit more than he was comfortable with, out of the sight of his friends waiting at the gate.

He tried to remain calm on the surface as he walked through, he didn't want to appear as if he was trying to hurry out of the yard.

As he walked he spotted the ball over near the wooden stockade fence, just under the chestnut tree. As He bent over to pick the ball up, BAM! He heard the sound of something hitting the fence.

He shifted his gaze and he saw a chestnut bounce off the fence and into the deep overgrowth.

He stood up sharply and turned towards the house, just as he did the screen door slammed shut and a strong wind blew toward him through the yard. He ran back towards the driveway and through the front gate…

"What happened back there?" one of the kids asked... "Man, if the ball goes over there again," he answered, "someone *else* is going to have to go get it."

A Childhood Ghost Story

This is a true haunting story, told to you, as it was told to me.

When Nancy Barragan was about 3 years old, the year was 1977 and she and her family had just moved into a house they had recently purchased in New England. The house was an old Victorian fixer-upper her dad had purchased with the intention of converting it into a three family dwelling in order to earn an income on the property.

Nancy recalls that the house was huge, boasting three floors of living space, the exterior was painted brown with yellow trim.

Natalie's father, a General Contractor and construction worker by trade, promptly began the remodel on the house. About this time, little Nancy began seeing various apparitions in the home, including 'people' walking into, out of and through her bedroom walls.

Most disturbing of all, she saw a frightened woman who appeared to be hanging by the neck and wearing a nightgown with a bathrobe thrown loosely over her.

She had long dark hair and a pale complexion. It was apparent to Natalie that the woman had been badly beaten, her face was disfigured, she could see there were bruises on her face and dried blood was caked into her hair, causing it to stick to the side of her head.

She remembers being deathly frightened at the appearance of the woman and screaming out for her parents, "My mother would be unable to move... frozen by the fear she could sense in the sounds of my screams."

Natalie recalled, "My parents were strict church-going Christians, they thought I was just having night-terrors." As the years progressed, things got worse for Nancy and the ghostly sightings became increasingly difficult to deal with.

Natalie says that the outbursts prompted her dad to turn her bedroom into an office, in hopes that moving her out of the room would bring an end to her night terrors. Conflict over the house may have contributed to rising tension between her parents, which inevitably caused them to split up. Nevertheless, Natalie and her siblings ended up moving to New York with their mother, leaving her father with the house in New England.

As she and her siblings got older, however, they would return and spend the summers with their dad.

It was during one of these visits, when Natalie was about 10 years old, that she saw the ghostly woman again, hanging in a corner of that same room, near the front of the house; only this time, the woman appeared to be reaching out towards her, as if calling to her.

She revealed this to her father who dismissed it as a figment of a child's overactive imagination. She says that after that she never told another person about the experiences or what she had seen.

Maybe her father was right, and besides, if her own father would not believe her, who else would believe a child? Right?

During another summer visit, while riding her bicycle in the neighborhood, Natalie got up the nerve to talk to a neighbor who lived about three houses away from her father's house.

She asked the woman if their home was haunted. "What makes you ask that?" the woman questioned. Nancy told her about hearing and feeling strange things in certain parts of the house, especially whenever she was there alone.

The woman told Nancy that a doctor lived in the house years ago with his sister and that the sister had died. A few years later the doctor sold the house to an investor and moved away.

Natalie says that another hotspot in the house was the basement where there was a game room, and that she watched pool balls roll around on their own, one shooting across the table violently, as if someone had thrown it, while no one else was there.

"When we all lived there together, even my mother refused to go into the basement alone," Natalie remembers. "You felt as if someone was at the bottom of the stairs waiting and watching you as you made your way down the steps."

She recalls that on one occasion, "When I was about 15, my father sent me down there to get some tools for him. While searching, I felt someone standing right behind me, breathing on the back of my neck! It was NOT a pleasant experience!"

Nancy says that she turned around only to find (as she suspected) that no one was there, but she remembers feeling a very strange sensation, something she could only describe as "extreme discomfort or oppression".

She said that it felt as if she was about to be sick.

"I went up those stairs as fast as I could - the door was stuck! I heard footsteps coming up the stairs behind me, I almost peed my pants... that is how frightened I was! The lights turned off; it was pitch black and I was screaming to be let out, banging on the door. I looked back and the lights turned back on and I noticed there was something leaking from the wall; it looked like blood to me. I yelled and freakin' pushed on that door and it suddenly opened. I ran upstairs, took a shower and tried to convince myself that it was just my imagination, like my dad had told me before."

"A few weeks before leaving, I saw the same woman hanging by her neck in the corner of the room. This time I was just fed up, thinking that this has got to stop. I decided to confront her. I asked her why she was bothering me and what hurt her so badly to make her kill herself."

That's when Natalie says that she actually experienced the woman's pain. "I sensed and saw what happened to her, she was brutally raped by 3 or 4 men and left for dead. In her agony and pain she decided to hang herself. After experiencing that, I never set foot into that house again!"

Natalie now lives in the same area that the house is located in, and it is still there. "Even today as I pass by the house there is something that draws me to look up at what once used to be my room, and I can still sense her there in the window, staring down at me."

In Closing

As we draw to the end of this work, I would like to reiterate that the work is never done. If we are to further the field and be taken seriously as researchers then we must incorporate elements of scientific methodology into our work.

We need to move away from the thrill seeking element that has become the prevailing image of the paranormal investigator. It does have its place, but there must be a clear distinctiveness between the researcher and the thrill seeker.

I have in as many cases as possible provided the possible scientific or logical explanation for many phenomena that are classified as paranormal or anomalous.

I do this not to disprove the possibility of seemingly inexplicable occurrences, but to show that in order for something to truly be classified as paranormal, all other explanations must be understood, taken into consideration and ruled out. *Knowledge goes a long way.

Our group will continue the work, and we hope to see more and more breakthroughs and doors kicked open for future researchers.

Glossary

Apparition- A supernatural appearance of a person or thing, especially a ghost; a specter or phantom; wraith: a ghostly apparition. anything that appears, especially something remarkable or startling.

Demonologist- One who studies Demons within a religious context, and in most cases, claims to have the ability to identify and expel demons in cases of possession or obsession.

Egregore- The word derives from the Greek word egrégoroi, meaning "watchers", which can also be transliterated as "grigori". Is best described as a "thoughtform" or "collective group mind," an autonomous psychic entity that is made up of, and is symbiotically influenced by the thoughts and beliefs of a group of people.

EMF- Electro-Magnetic Fields are an area through which energy passes that has been created by electrically charged particles. EMFs are caused by man-made things such as power lines, electrical appliances, radio waves, and microwaves; they also occur naturally, in instances such as thunder and lightning storms as well as the earth's own magnetic fields.

Evocation- In ritual or prayer, the act of intentionally calling or inviting a spirit or entity to be present. To call forth.

Invocation- In ritual or prayer, the act of calling or inviting a spirit or entity into one's body. To call in.

EVP- Electronic Voice Phenomena are recordings of voice, or voice-like sounds and answers that are typically captured when someone uses a recording device such as a digital voice recorder, that can be heard upon playback. The frequencies of these sounds are reportedly below the range of sounds that can be perceived by the human ear.

Future-Life Progression- Future life progression works on the same principles as past life regression, except in reverse; that is, one is "moved forward" through present time and shown glimpses of lives to come.

Past-Life Regression- Based on the techniques used by modern psychologists to perform regression therapy, that is, moving the subject backward through their subconscious memory to a previous time in their lives, usually childhood, to find the root cause of an issue; past life regression moves the subject backwards in time beyond this present life, into one from the past.

Golem: A golem is most widely known as an artificial creature made of inanimate material which has been animated by magical means, often to serve its creator. The word golem comes from a Hebrew word that means shapeless mass.

Haunting- is the inhabitation of a location, or visitation by a ghost or spectre.

Intelligent Haunting- The entity or spirit interacts with the living and maybe tries to communicate. Interacts with and appears to be aware of the environment.

Kabbalah- an esoteric tradition that seeks to understand God's essence, the relationship between God and the world, and the inner meaning of the Torah. Kabbalah is often practiced through study, contemplation, and mystical experiences.

Residual Haunting- Unintelligent hauntings, said to be like recordings replaying a scene or event from the past. Does not interact or seem aware of the living or the environment.

Pareidolia (Matrixing)- is a phenomena where one sees likenesses or images in random or ambiguous patterns (like seeing faces, animals or other shapes in clouds). In psychology it is considered to be a form of Apophenia (a human tendency to unreasonably seek definite patterns and connections in random, unrelated information).

RSPK: Recurrent Spontaneous Psychokinesis-(poltergeist activity)- The ability (consciously or unconsciously) to influence or move physical objects without physical contact. When this is done intentionally it is generally called telekinesis, when it occurs without control it is referred to as spontaneous psychokinesis, like in the movie Carrie.

Shadow Person- Is described as an entity with density. They are generally described as featureless dark masses. There are several classifications of shadow people, and usually they are associated with feelings of dread and fear.

Their forms are said to be palpable enough to block light, meaning you can't see through them, nor does light pass through their forms.

Sigil- Similar to a talisman, but can be worn for a number of reasons; to attract or repel certain energies or circumstances, protection, to attract a mate or financial gain are a few.

Unlike talismans sigils are usually created by the wearer and are believed to be more powerful because they are usually charged or imbued with the intent of the one wearing it.

Harry Price- January 1881 - March 1948 was a London born Paranormal Researcher who achieved great public recognition for his work in the realm of psychic phenomena investigation.

He became a member of SPR in 1920, and also had a working knowledge of conjuring and "black magic'" which he used at times to debunk mediums and explain the circumstances surrounding certain events.

Spirit Board (Ouija)- is a flat board marked with the letters of the alphabet, the numbers 0-9, the words "yes", "no" and "goodbye", along with various symbols and graphics. It uses a movable indicator to communicate messages by spelling them out on the board.

Stigmata- Are bodily marks, sores, or sensations of pain in locations corresponding to the crucifixion wounds of Jesus Christ, such as the hands and feet. In some cases, rope marks on the wrists have accompanied the wounds on the hands.

Talisman- an object, usually religious, held to act as a charm to avert evil and bring good fortune: something producing apparently magical or miraculous effects. A Christian cross can be an example of a talisman.

White Noise- Is a sound that contains all frequencies within the spectrum of audible sound in equal parts. Similar to water running or static. White noise is utilized in paranormal investigations for the purpose of trying to collect EVP's, though this can work similarly to matrixing except with hearing, sometimes referred to as Auditory Pareidolia.

Plasma or Ectoplasm- A viscous substance believed to be secreted or otherwise exteriorized by psychics and mediums as a result of the manifestation of a spirit. Many examples of ectoplasm can be found in researching old photographs of mediums at work.

Today plasm is more-so recognized among some paranormal researchers as appearing as a wisp of smoke or steam, generally showing up in photographs.